5.95

To m...

+ Jane

4-25-69

Remember with Me

RUTH LYONS
Remember with Me

Introduction by John T. Murphy

1969

DOUBLEDAY & COMPANY, INC.
GARDEN CITY, NEW YORK

Grateful acknowledgment is made to Alice Kennelly
Roberts for permission to reprint "In Memory of Miss
Candy Newman," which appeared in her column "Rime
'n' Reason," in the *Cincinnati Enquirer*.

To My Beloved Candy
and
Her Devoted Father

Contents

●●●

Introduction

For nearly 21 years, Ruth Lyons' 50-50 CLUB opened the windows of the world to her countless viewers and listeners.

Those years were truly something special in the Midwest cities where her show was broadcast—and they were very special for Avco Broadcasting.

To the thousands of Midwest housewives who tuned her television or radio show in daily, Ruth Lyons was every bit as real, and as loved, as a member of their family. She stretched their minds and their horizons. Ofttimes she infuriated, as well as fascinated, her audiences, because controversy was something from which she never backed away. She was "with it"—whether the subject was "putting up" pickles . . . politics . . . the Cincinnati Reds . . . medicine . . . superstitions . . . travel . . . religion . . . or SHOW BUSINESS. Ruth loved show business and its people, and her own program became known from coast to coast as a favorite stopping off place for nearly all the top names whenever they were near this area.

This was a lady who could sell soap for the family wash as if she spent half her life with her arms in suds up to the elbows. Yet she traveled the world and mingled with the mighty. Her enthusiasm knew no bounds. It was as great for the soap she was selling as for the travel she loved.

Ruth's office staff and co-workers on the show were a fiercely loyal lot. She was "Mother" to them all, and would fight like a tigress if she suspected any one of them had been treated unfairly.

Comets like Ruth Lyons don't often cross the entertainment sky. When they do, they never leave it quite the same. She was, indeed, the single individual most responsible for putting Avco Broadcasting solidly and squarely into a commitment to local live programing. The depth of that commitment is unique in the world of local television. No other broadcaster, so far as we know, does as much regular big budget local live programing as does Avco Broadcasting.

Ruth Lyons proved to us, as others have since, that there is an excitement—a vitality—a warmth and audience empathy —and a sponsor loyalty—in local live shows no other type of programing can match.

Any remarks about Ruth Lyons would have to include mention of the tremendous good that has been done with the Ruth Lyons Christmas Fund. Her dedication to this cause transcended consideration for her own health, and her own personal heartbreak. Since her retirement, Avco Broadcasting and 50-50 CLUB have been proud to carry on this good work in her name.

She will tell you about the Christmas Fund in her book. But her words may be too modest to express the lifelong appreciation of grateful parents . . . the smile brought to each wan little face of a hospitalized child . . . when he received his own special toy from the Ruth Lyons Christmas Fund. Many of these young patients are now grown and parents themselves, but they have never forgotten the touch of happiness Ruth Lyons gave to an apprehensive moment of their childhood.

This, then, is her story, told in her own words for the first time. It is the story of a woman who loved children, and especially her own lovely Candy; who made millions happy with her music and entertainment; and who made a conversation show famous in the Midwest long before "talk shows" were fashionable. And while Ruth and her own personal magic have now retired from the airwaves, she blazed a way of programing that lives on today in the vast areas reached by WLW Radio and Television stations.

JOHN T. MURPHY, *President*
AVCO *Broadcasting Corporation*

chapter one
My Childhood

Now that I am no longer before the public, I finally have time to sit back and try to recall the many experiences of my life, some happy, some sad, but many beautiful. It is amazing all the things that come back to one, the bits and pieces that make up the patchwork of a life. When I first began this book, I wondered what it should be called. I must try to remember so many, many things, and who remembers many of them better than you, my loyal audience, perhaps better than I. So let us recall these things together, for you, the audience, were a great part of my life. And although you have heard me tell many of the stories before, both on radio and TV especially, and have met most of the wonderful guests, when I told you thousands of things I had experienced, you always seemed eager for more. Perhaps as you read on, you too will *Remember with Me*. I hope so.

I was born in Cincinnati, Ohio, at the age of five, on a bright October afternoon, just two hours after my mother had finished sweeping the front porch. It has always surprised me that I did not come into this world carrying a baseball bat and wearing a straw hat. Yes, I must have been at least five years at birth, because everyone has always added five or ten years to my age ever since. I reached twenty-nine years of age twenty-eight years ago, and I am still the same age today.

My only sister was born in June four and a half years later. I adored her and wanted to name her Dorothy, but my mother chose Rose Jane, after a dear friend of hers.

We had a family life filled with all the ordinary experiences of the times. One afternoon, when I was just a tot, my mother took me to town on a trolley car for some shopping. One of the great delights was to stand up on the seat and look out. This also prevented car sickness in that day, which every mother of young children dreaded. On this particular day I insisted on standing up on the opposite side of the car from my mother. The seats ran lengthwise in those days. All at once my mother let out a scream as I leaned out the window. Not because I was about to fall, but because she discovered that beneath my very stiffly starched dress and petticoat, she had forgotten to put on my panties. She tried to get me to sit down, but I could not be persuaded. Naturally our first stop was in the children's department of a store.

It seemed that I always loved music. When I was three years old, my mother would place me upon the table while she was ironing and teach me songs, which I never forgot, and would sing them later without being asked. I started to take piano lessons when I was six years old. My teacher was a prim, middle-aged lady, who sat beside her pupils and rapped their fingers with a pencil when they were prone to "syncopate," as I was disposed to do. I remember one recital to which our proud parents were subjected. She insisted that we use our music and that the program proceed just as a lesson, with her sitting beside each pupil. It so happened that a sudden spring storm came up just as it was time for me to perform. The wind blew wildly through the open win-

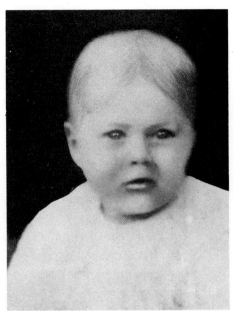

Here I am
at the age of one.

And at six years,
with the flowers
I have always loved.

dow, and right in the middle of "Shepherd's Evening Song," my music was wafted across the platform. It didn't disturb me in the least, and I continued to play on while my teacher spent the next three minutes on her hands and knees, trying to catch the elusive music. The applause was great, whether for me or for the agility displayed by my teacher's acrobatics.

I always had a vivid imagination, which in many instances stood me in good stead. In our home there was a very long staircase, complete with a marvelous banister and uprights on every step. Every Saturday I was given the job of thoroughly dusting it, for which I received ten cents, later a quarter. So the Tom Sawyer in me was used to good advantage. I would encourage my friends as co-workers to help me, offering as a reward some penny candy. Then I would sit at the top of the stairs, and while they toiled I would regale them with fascinating stories. My mother couldn't understand why it took so long to do the staircase, but the stories were dragged out and added to every week. Thus was inaugurated the first "soap opera."

Later, as I grew older, and my allowance reached the tremendous sum of twenty-five cents, I took one of my helpers each week to Keith's vaudeville. The only stipulation was they had to pay their own carfare, five cents each way. How we looked forward to these Saturday afternoons! I came home week after week with a new song in my head which I then picked out on the piano. Of course, I couldn't remember the words, so my father would go to the Song Shop on the following Monday and buy me the sheet music. It always amazed me that invariably the song would be written in the very same key that I had remembered it and played it in. And so, I discovered, not then, but later, that I had "perfect pitch." A B-Flat to me could be nothing but a B-Flat.

I walked a mile each way to school every day. Sometimes I roller-skated. I always loved school, and I had some wonderful teachers. In the fourth grade I played my first thespian role. I was the eldest daughter in *Mrs. Wiggs of the Cabbage Patch*. You may recall the Wiggses were very poor, but Mrs. Wiggs always tried to be proper in everything she did. We were invited to visit the big house on the hill, and there was quite a problem as to what we should wear. I can still remember the mother admonishing us to be sure we each had a clean handkerchief pinned to our dresses—but the matter of getting a hat for everyone was impossible. So we were told over and over again that when we arrived and were asked to "lay our hats aside," I, being the eldest, should speak up and say, "It was such a pleasant evening and such a short walk that we thought we'd leave our hats to home." These were my first words to an audience. Somehow, it came out, "It was such a short evening and such a pleasant hat that we thought we'd leave our walks to home." My mother nearly died of humiliation when the audience laughed, but I was not a bit upset. These were my first words on the stage, but as events proved later, they were far from my last.

Our life centered around the Sixth Presbyterian Church. We attended five services each Sunday—Sunday School, Morning Service, Afternoon Christian Endeavor, Regular Christian Endeavor, and Evening Service, plus church suppers and special Christmas and Easter programs. There were also choir rehearsals and even Billy Sunday's "Sawdust Trail Campaigns." Speaking of Billy Sunday, he had a handsome trombone player named Homer Rodeheaver, who later, when I was in radio and television, was one of my most ardent fans.

Those church suppers were really something. They always ended in someone not speaking to someone else. You see, each good lady had a specialty, and woe unto anyone who usurped her prerogative to perform it. Mrs. Hodge always mashed the potatoes, and no one else. My grandmother was always in charge of making the gravy. My mother and several others took charge of opening the cans of peas or corn and dishing them up. No one else liked the pies or cakes, except us kids, for every good soul thought she could have improved on them with her own special recipe.

Another bone of contention was the church Christmas play. There was always a fairy queen in it (why, I don't remember), and the year my pretty, rather plump cousin Mary was chosen for the part, she dissolved into tears and could not go on. One of the boys had said she looked, not like the fairy queen, but more like the *Island Queen,* the big stern-wheeler that we rode every summer on a trip to Coney Island. The Christmas pageants were discontinued after my cousin Bud and his chum hid behind the crepe-paper fireplace, and at a very inopportune moment, lost their balance and crashed through onto the stage—in full view. Pandemonium reigned.

My grandfather was a chief elder of the church, my father led the choir, my uncles, George and Jim, were soloists, and I played the piano and organ. As chief elder, it was my grandfather's duty, with the help of my grandmother, to prepare the communion. My grandmother baked the unleavened bread, washed the individual glasses for the grape juice which filled them, and then on Communion Sunday carried them all to the church. On the back of every pew was a small rack in which to place the glasses after the solemn ritual was performed. My grandfather was delighted when my cousin Bud and I offered to collect the glasses after service was over, until he happened to discover one Sunday that we were draining the dregs of the grape juice. That ended that.

My grandparents on my mother's side both died when I was very young, so my memory of them is quite indistinct.

However, my grandmother on my father's side was greatly beloved by me and had a great influence on me. She was a remarkable woman. She arose every morning, winter and summer, at four o'clock. By nine o'clock, her housework all completed, she dressed in a neat black dress and hat and did her marketing. Then she called on my mother, my aunt, and her own mother, who lived to be eighty-six years old. She would also take food to many of the poor families. In the afternoon her immaculately kept house was always open to one and all. She had very strong convictions. Although she and my grandfather when they were courting, had been great dancers, upon joining the church she gave up dancing and she never saw a movie or a stage play in her life. But she read every newspaper and magazine available and was quite well informed. She was a charter member of the Cincinnati WCTU, and fought constantly with the saloonkeepers, who tempted the men from the local sawmill to spend their weekly wages at their bars every Saturday night, and therefore kept their families in need. Her watchword was "God, Country, and Sobriety." During World War I when the Turks were massacring the Armenians, she happened to see an ad in the newspaper for Camel cigarettes. At that time, it showed a picture of a camel being led by a Turkish sheik. My outraged grandmother, knowing nothing of ad agencies or the like, wrote a letter immediately to the president of the company who manufactured the cigarettes. Somehow, the letter reached the president, and she received an answer saying that he completely agreed with her. From then on a lonely camel has been displayed on the package for which, "Men walk a mile."

There was at that time a saloon owned by a Mr. Pat Bain. One day my grandmother called on him and explained the plight of the families of the men that frequented his establishment each Saturday night. She must have put up a very good case, for from then on he limited his customers to several beers each. Later on he often called on my grandmother and came to her funeral when she died.

I was amused recently while driving out the modern parkway, which has now replaced many of the old homes and roads of my childhood, to see one exit bearing the sign Bain's Place.

My participation in the First World War effort made me the greatest perpetrator of dental cavities. Each day I rushed home from school to make several varieties of fudge, which I sold to the neighbors, and donated the proceeds to the Red Cross. My father's bill at the grocery was enormous, and I borrowed sugar wherever possible. Everyone in the neighborhood was eager to help by lending me sugar. Chocolate fudge was the best seller, maple the poorest, and I have hated maple-filled chocolates ever since. My father held a large carnival at the school; all proceeds went to the Red Cross.

The Fourth of July was truly a celebration for us all. We always had homemade lemon sherbet. In the afternoon, there was a great ceremony, when my father, Uncle George and Uncle Jim sent up paper balloons. Do you remember that type of balloon? They were about ten feet tall, red, white, and blue, and at the bottom opening there was a disc of excelsior, which when lighted caused the air inside the balloon to expand and thus set sail to the balloon. In our neighborhood the balloons were supposed to sail out over the river. That was what was meant to happen, but often the result was quite the opposite. Either the balloon caught fire before it ever got off the ground, or if there was a successful launching, it often ended by dropping onto a nearby roof top. Eventually, this type of celebration was banned because of the fire hazard. In the evening, the entire neighborhood tried to outdo one another in the skyrockets, pinwheels, Roman candles, and sparklers. One Fourth of July when I was about six, Cousin Bud, who was just nine months older than I, decided to decorate the entire front yard with sparklers by sticking them in the ground. It was quite a job getting them all lit at one time, and in hurrying to do so, my skirt brushed against one of them and I soon was enveloped in flames. My father, never far away when there was any form of fire, ripped my dress and petticoat completely off. His hands were badly burned, but I had just a small burn on my right arm. I also had on just the yoke to my dress. For years my mother saved that charred memento symbolic of the dangers of the Fourth.

My father had a morbid fear of fire. In those days the Christmas trees had real candles, and the lighting of it each year was quite an event. All during my childhood I thought that part of the tree trimming was a large pail of water standing beside it, and it wasn't until many years later that I ever saw a completely lighted Christmas tree. By the time my father succeeded in getting the last candle lit, the first ones had to be extinguished. The candles were small and burned very quickly, and no one, but no one, was permitted to assist my father in this dangerous task.

When I was in the eighth grade I wrote my first musical play, designed the sets and crepe-paper costumes, and had the leading role, that of a wildflower, rather than the more exotic flowers, such as lilies, orchids, and roses. The only complaint came from one mother whose daughter wore a purple costume to represent a pansy, which color the mother vehemently proclaimed did not become her daughter at all. Mine was pink with green leaves. The whole point of the story was that the meek little wildflower, despite her lowly estate, won the heart of the prince.

We worry today about school children excelling and mak-

My father and mother, Samuel Spencer Reeves and Margaret K. Reeves.

ing good grades. Well, my last year in elementary school was beyond belief. There were four of us striving for highest honors—three boys and I. We were graded in those days with "E" for Excellent, "VG" for Very Good, "G" for Good, "P" for Poor, and "F" for Failure. After the third report card we were so close in our grades that we were all in line to receive the Mercantile Library card, which entitled the winner to a year's access to a special library downtown. And what could the teacher do to differentiate between all the E pluses we had amassed? She finally decided that the only solution was to give double E's to those who earned them. How we studied and worried over that final report card! I won with double E's in every subject, and was awarded the library card. I never used it once, and to this day I have never been in the Mercantile Library. And so ended my grade school days. They were happy, wonderful days, full of friendliness and excitement, and I looked forward with great anticipation to going to high school.

chapter two

My High School Days

I was scheduled to attend a brand new high school, East High, the name of which was later changed to Withrow High. It was a beautiful school with a tall bell tower in front and a small bridge leading from the street. The day I crossed that bridge for the first time was a tremendous thrill. Inside, many of the interior appointments were not yet finished. This caused a great deal of confusion and also merriment on the part of all of us newcomers. The lockers, which had not been installed, lined the lower halls. The chemistry lab was merely a lot of pipes sticking up out of the floor. There was a long tunnel leading from the main building to the gymnasium.

I took a college preparatory course including Latin, English, algebra, and general science. And immediately I became involved in all the musical activities. I played the accompaniment for the boys in Glee Club and the special chorus, and played violin in the senior orchestra; I was pianist for the day dancing classes and two dancing classes at night for adults, for which I was paid. The money I received helped me to pay for a few little extras. The music director was a delightful little man named Mr. Joseph Surdo. He was Italian and taught in the Cincinnati school system for over sixty years. While we learned a great deal from him, he was the butt of all the trickery of which teenagers can be guilty. Two musical classes a week were compulsory, but as a general rule only one was held, for the music room had to be fumigated from the "stink bombs" tossed in by various and sundry members of the "unmusical" students. No guilty person was ever caught.

Once I was guilty of wrongdoing. The junior orchestra needed a viola player, and Mr. Surdo arranged for me to have that dubious job. The viola was furnished by the school, and I took lessons from Jean ten Have, with whom I also studied violin. I hated the viola, mostly I think because its carrying case was a large wooden box painted black. Week after week I would pretend to forget to bring the viola for practice. Mr. Surdo stood this for just so long, and then one Friday he demanded that I go home and get it after school was out and return for rehearsal. I lived quite a distance from the school, and at that time there was some repair work being done on the streetcar line that I usually took. It was necessary for me to go all the way to town, change cars there for my home, pick up the viola, then return by the same route. I dallied and had a snack at home before I returned. When I got back to the school, it was six o'clock and all the doors were locked tightly. My punishment was that Mr. Surdo would not release me from the junior orchestra, and I suffered through two more years of carrying that hateful, black wooden box.

Years later, when I was on WLW television, I mentioned that Mr. Surdo was celebrating his ninetieth birthday, and knowing that he had inspired thousands of school children in this area, I asked my audience to send him birthday cards. I was delighted to hear that he had received more than five thousand cards and notes, which pleased him greatly.

I hated general science, and barely managed to get through it. The teacher had no love for me either, and it was she who caused my most embarrassing experience during my first year. Our general science class was held just prior to lunchtime. One day as we rushed from her class to the lunchroom, I felt something let go—the rubber in the waistband of my gym bloomers, which we wore under our pleated skirts. I quickly ran behind some of the new lockers, still not installed, and despite her pleading, stayed there. But that staunch custodian of test tubes was not to be denied, and thinking that I was trying to play hookey for the rest of the day, held up the line of starving students and demanded that I come out of hiding. I refused vehemently, but she was as determined as I. And when she finally threatened to send for the principal, I gave up, and stepping out of my bloomers, and with them draped over my arm, came forth. That was the end of my science career.

During my sophomore, junior, and senior years, I elected to take Spanish instead of any more science courses. I continued with Latin for four years, a choice which I have never regretted. In my senior year I took astronomy and geology, thinking that the night classes would be quite exciting, but they were very disappointing, for few romances developed. During my senior year I was elected co-editor of the annual yearbook and wrote and performed in my first musical. We had formed a group, the Kalidasa Club, under the aegis of our wonderful Spanish teacher, Miss Aldrich. She encouraged us to plan the musical. However, I soon learned that the school board frowned on any such venture. I contacted the principal, who said his hands were tied also. Then I marched down to call on the superintendent of schools and used all my persuasion to get his permission to put on the musical show. He finally consented.

The musical was a great success, and became the fore-runner of *The Sounds of Withrow*, a tremendous talent show which is still well known city-wide.

My last year of high school was indeed hectic. I had so much detention for talking in class and other misdemeanors and very often being late to classes, that I had to invent many excuses to avoid being marked "tardy." I believe the most farfetched one was the morning I told our school adviser that on my way to school a milk truck had upset and the poor milkman had a dreadful task of retrieving the many bottles scattered all over the street. Feeling sorry for him, I had gotten off of the streetcar to help him pick up many bottles. As a result I was compelled to wait a half hour for the next streetcar to come along. Whether she believed me I cannot say, but with her eyes twinkling, she excused my late arrival at school.

My father had pneumonia during that final year, and he was very ill for a long time. The doctor who attended him lived just a block away. Every morning I went to see the doctor and asked about my father, which accounted for much of my tardy arrival at school. You see, I was afraid he wasn't telling my mother the true facts about my father's condition. The doctor finally said that he worried more about me than he did about my father, who was ill for four months. I was concerned inasmuch as the woman next door, who was much older than my father, had come down with the same ailment several days prior to my father's illness. Yet she was up and walking about in six weeks, while it took my father over four months to recuperate. It seems she had an osteopathic phy-sician treating her. This experience contributed to my lifelong interest in and support of the osteopathic profession.

Each Friday afternoon during my last year of high school I went with the minister of our church to play for those confined in the Home for the Incurables. This was most depressing for me, but I managed to include it among my many other activities. I was compelled to arrive at school one hour early and stay overtime to make up all the detention I had acquired. I got out of some of it by rehearsing after school the musical I had written, for which I played all the accompaniments and wrote the script. But I rather liked coming early, and the janitor, who had to let me in, became one of my best friends. During high school I made many new friends, and I became very fond of many of my teachers. I finally won my diploma and the gift of a gold filigree watch from my mother and father, and having taken all the tests successfully, I was enrolled at the University of Cincinnati.

During the summer after graduation we moved because of my father's health and the long streetcar ride he had to make back and forth from Madisonville, a suburb of Cincinnati.

Before we moved, I decided I simply could not live any longer without owning a bicycle. My mother always opposed my having one, although I rode one belonging to the boy across the street. So I had to evolve a plot. The opportunity came in connection with our moving. One Saturday afternoon when my mother went to see the new house, I decided to help her lighten the moving load. We had a very large porch, and my sister and I and Trevor, the boy across the street, strung a rope across the porch and began to hang up pots and pans and old dresses we thought we no longer needed. We also posted a large sign FOR SALE. And Trevor mounted his bike and rode forth to spread the news of the sale around the neighborhood. We had resounding success and began to run out of saleable merchandise. So we added several of my mother's dresses and hats, and as a last resort my sister and I decided that my mother's winter coat was very unbecoming to her. But someone liked it, for it brought ten dollars. In all, the sale netted us $28.50, plus the worst scolding my mother and father had ever administered to me. And the worst blow of all, the $28.50 was appropriated by them to help pay the moving bill.

chapter three

My College Days

So, with no bicycle, but high hopes, I entered college. I loved the University of Cincinnati and immediately became enmeshed in campus activities. We played bridge every lunch hour, a game that I still love. At the very beginning there was the "rush" for sororities. My reputation for activities had preceded me, and I was welcomed by six sororities. Next door to me lived a Theta Phi Alpha, across the street, another Theta. One of my closest friends was a Kappa Kappa Gamma. Because her mother had also been a member, she was influenced by legacy (Whatever my mother is, I must be!) to choose this sorority. Two of my close friends and I chose Delta Delta Delta. Soon thereafter, we decided to organize an independent group uniting old high school friends. This caused great consternation to the Dean of Women, but we persevered. We called this the "Checker Board Society." We chose three freshmen from each of the six leading sororities. We had great fun and a sense of camaraderie that was left over from high school days.

I must have had a guardian angel hovering over me that first year. There was a wonderful family, of which four daughters were at the university; one of the daughters, Betty,

I enter college.

was a great friend of mine. It was my habit to ride home from school with them and their father every day.

One Friday afternoon I felt like skipping my biology lab class, as I had a headache. I told Betty, and she asked if she might borrow my new felt hat to wear on a date that night. It was the custom then, as I'm sure it still is, to trade formals, coats, and hats with one's best friends. I gave the hat to Betty and left school. Imagine my horror to learn that evening that their car had been struck by a train at a crossing which we made every night and that Betty and one of her sisters and her father were killed. The other sister in the car was seriously injured; the fourth one had stayed at school to make up some work. And as I, who departed early, she too was spared. It was a tragedy, I shall never forget.

In college I studied French, which I loved. However, although I can still read it fairly well, I cannot speak a word of it. (I think this is one of the great errors in the method by which languages are taught. I'm afraid it still continues in most public colleges.)

I won the first prize in music on Honors Day by writing a plaintive little song titled, "Great White Moon"; later I wrote nearly the entire score for the musical produced each year by the Fresh Painters, which ran for a week at a downtown theatre. This was not too easy for me to do, as the words had already been written, while I found it easier to write both the music and lyrics when composing. The big number in the show was "Bungalow Blues," which was sung by Libby Holman and is reputed to be her first blues number. She has since sung many more blues songs on Broadway and become a well-known star, but it all began at the University of Cincinnati. The musical was a light, frothy, typical college production, called *Lemme Alone*. I did not take part in the musical, but I certainly enjoyed seeing it performed.

All during my first year, I tutored a high school boy four nights a week and on Sunday afternoons. His father had promised him a car of his own if he made passing grades, and the father was willing to pay to help him. It was a lovely family, and they treated me very kindly in their home. In later years when I was on television, this same wonderful boy, now grown and president of a large company in Cincinnati, never failed to send a thousand dollar contribution to the Ruth Lyons' Christmas Fund.

It is a strange thing, but my first encounter with snobbery, intolerance, and prejudice came while I was a university student. While working on the music of the Fresh Painters, I met a very fine Jewish boy. He was a wonderful musician and very handsome. He invited me to a dance at school, and I accepted gladly. Later, when talking with some of my older sorority sisters, I mentioned with whom I was going. You cannot imagine what a crisis they made of it! But I went anyway, and enjoyed the evening thoroughly.

I wrote a new Tri Delta song, a sweetheart song for Sigma Alpha Epsilon, and many skits and musical numbers for other occasions. As a freshman I was appointed humor editor of *The Cincinnatian,* the yearbook. When I look back at it all now, I wonder how I did all I did without completely collapsing.

There were other dramatic instances which occurred from time to time. One such was when I proposed a girl to be a member of Delta Delta Delta and found to my surprise that she was unacceptable because her mother and father had been divorced ten years before. However, I delivered my final blow for tolerance at the last meeting of Delta Delta Delta that I attended. It seems, that after all other disbursements had been made, there still remained twenty-five dollars in the treasury. The Catherine Booth Home for unwed mothers was considered, pro and con, to be the recipient. I finally arose and said, "I move the twenty-five dollars be given to the Catherine Booth Home, for who can tell which one of us may some day need it." And it was so ordered!

In my days in college the sororities and fraternities personified, with a few exceptions, real snobbery. They have moved slowly along the path of tolerance, but their history of heartbreak and disappointment for many in the past is not forgotten.

The first vacation summer was an unforgettable one. We lived not too far from Lunken Airport, and many of the student pilots roomed near us. And so we became very interested in flying, or that is to say, the pilots. I shiver now to think of the chances we took in the air at that time. The planes were very small and not too well conditioned. The most frightening were the first Aeroncas, especially when you looked out the side, which just wasn't there. It was like flying in an oversized cracker box. One Sunday afternoon I took a ride with one of the instructors whose plane was slightly larger, and I felt very safe even when he did spirals and flew upside down, showing off all the tricks of the trade. However, the very next Sunday he flew to Indiana to drop flowers on his mother's grave; he suffered a heart attack and crashed his plane. That ended my desire to fly. I have traveled the world over, but I have never been in an airplane since.

We played tennis nearly every day and went dancing every night. The boys I had met in college were very attentive. Now, some of them are lawyers, doctors, psychiatrists, and businessmen all over the country.

I earned money that first summer by tutoring the boy next door in French. He had failed his high school course and was given the chance to make up his grades so that he might pass that year. I studied one lesson ahead of him each day, and on the day of his exam, no mother could have worried more about how he was doing. He made it!

My mother always wanted me to become a teacher. My father, who had worked for the railroad as a rate expert, was a living computer. He served on President Hoover's committee to send food to Europe. Then he started the travel bureau in one of the large banks in Cincinnati and taught at night at the University of Cincinnati. However, that summer his health was not too good. I began to worry about the expense of another year at college, so I went off to that first day of fall registration, full of doubt, and feeling that I should start earning my own way. For two days I debated with myself. School seemed so futile, so meaningless, and I simply could not envision spending another year just having fun. I met one of my best friends, and I told him I thought I would try to get a job. He laughed, and asked me what kind of job I could get. After thinking it over, I realized that music was the one thing I knew best. So I did not register, but went to town, where the first place I applied for a job was the Willis Music Company. It was the custom in those days for all the music stores to have a pianist to play anything the customer wanted to hear. Such was the case at the Willis Music Company, owned then by the Schirmer Music Publishing Company. I marched into the offices there and asked for a job. They were very doubtful of my ability to succeed, since we were required to sell music as well as play the piano. However, one of the girls who was working there was leaving to be married, and I was finally told that I might have the job on a trial basis. I left there floating on Cloud Nine, but it still remained for me to break the news at home and to my sorority sisters.

I don't know who took it the hardest, my mother and

father or my sorority. The national president of Tri Delta came to Cincinnati and offered me a scholarship to continue school, but now I was determined to keep the job and to become independent. My mother and father were finally reconciled.

And that first job changed the course of my entire life. I worked very hard to prove that I was capable of doing the job which I had gotten. I was surprised to find that many of the members of the Cincinnati Symphony liked popular music as well as classical. I met many wonderful people. The concertmeister of the Cincinnati Symphony would come in regularly and have me play the entire score from *No, No, Nannette,* which included "Tea for Two." I sold hundreds of copies of "Lady Be Good," "Tea for Two," "Indian Love Call," and favorites from current musicals. In addition, I assisted the devoted nuns who bought all of the music there for their music classes. I also met a young tenor, Howard Hafford, who had the most divine tenor voice I have ever heard. He sang in various choirs and synagogues around town and was in great demand to entertain at private parties. One day he rushed into the store and asked me to sight-read a number for him entitled "The Devil's Love Song." It was written in six sharps, a most difficult key. I started to play it for him, making as few mistakes as possible, while he and others who worked in the store doubled up in laughter behind my back. Finally, when I reached a particularly difficult passage, I got up from the piano and told him that I didn't believe the number was suitable for him. From that day on we became good friends, and he asked me to become his accompanist. This meant that I received twenty-five and often fifty dollars for a few hours' work in the finest homes in Cincinnati.

But as usual, I tried to do too much, and after a year and a half I became ill and took a few months off.

I had always been an avid reader, and since we lived next door to the manager of the public library, I got a job there. I was going to be a full-fledged librarian. I worked in the library for a year, and then I had to take an exam for a promotion. The exam lasted for one full day and a half and covered, it seemed, everything ever written. On Friday, I was told that I was one of the four out of twenty-four who had passed and that I should report the following Monday for an assignment to the class just starting the school librarian's course. That first morning proved to me that I didn't want to be a librarian. I looked around at the class—at the frustrated appearance of the others, and I thought, "This is not for me." So at noon I went across the street to the bank to see my father and tell him that I had left the library. He was puzzled, but since he was shorthanded in the travel department, he asked if I would like to work there. I agreed most emphatically, for I would have every Saturday afternoon free to go to the Shubert Theatre. My father was a good friend of the manager, Nelson Trowbridge, and received free tickets for all the big shows and musicals that played in Cincinnati. And I got the day off whenever I wished to attend the stock company performances at the Cox Theatre. There I saw Spring Byington, Victor Jory, and many others who later became famous, who were permanent members of the Stuart Walker Players.

About this time I became aware of radio. WSAI was then owned by the U. S. Playing Card Company. Every Saturday night there was a program. Mr. Howard Hafford was a soloist, which incidentally was sponsored by the evening newspaper, the *Times-Star*. I also realized that I could transpose music very easily, and I began to accompany Norine Gibbons, an early favorite in Cincinnati radio, who needed all of her songs transposed to a lower key.

To appear on Saturday night radio was more like going to a party than anything else. They always served fruit punch from a big punch bowl outside the studio door. One night this proved to be a catastrophe for a member of the orchestra. The leading trumpeter was to play the "Carnival of Venice" that night, and just as he was ready to go into his triple tonguing, the announcer entered the studio and stood directly in front of him, sucking a huge lemon. You can well imagine the results.

My mother had a crystal set, and she spent half the night moving the "cat whisker" around trying to bring in various programs. Never once did she hear me. It was indeed frustrating to the two of us, and I was certain that radio was just a passing fancy.

However, I soon learned differently when one day I ran into Mr. Hafford, who had just been made music director of WKRC. He insisted on my reporting for work the following Monday to take over the job of cataloguing the music library there. Thus was the start of thirty-seven years before the microphone and later the television cameras.

chapter four

WKRC

When I went to WKRC, the station was an individually owned one, carrying Columbia Network programs. The first day I entered the doors of the WKRC studios, I nearly turned around and walked out. The music library that I was supposed to organize comprised stacks of music in every corner of the two studios. There was one large cupboard that was to be the library when finished. Across the hall, records were piled sky-high. To find a particular piece of music or a certain record was almost impossible. I was given a desk, just inside the door, from which I operated, and I began to try to bring order out of complete chaos.

First, let me tell you a bit about the people who then worked there. They were really kookey, but also very lovable. One, Duane Snodgrass, was an excellent pianist, a truly talented boy. I began to make friends and take part in many of the zany things that went on. And go on they did! I played accompaniment for some of the singers, and I loved to play the organ, which was often used as a music-fill at the close of a network show. Every morning we would gather around the control room to listen to a little-known disc jockey from Washington, D.C., by the name of Arthur Godfrey.

One morning in May 1929 the girl who presented "A Woman's Hour" show became ill, and since I was the only woman around besides the switchboard operator, I was told to go into the small studio and read the script, which she had prepared the day before. An announcer sat opposite me, and the engineer was peering through a glass window. I was petrified. There was one commercial message, and the rest was just commentary. Before the show I read it over and over again, and found it very boring. But I entered the studio telling myself that this was just for a day. However, when I was given the cue to begin, I said good morning to the announcer and also to the engineer, and then I rattled on about everything and anything that came into my mind. The script was forgotten, and I felt as though I was talking to people out there in radio land, who were interested in as many things as I was. The announcer nearly fainted, and the engineer was dumbstruck. When it was all over, I was sent for by the manager. He told me that the sponsor had called and would like for me to do the show every day. I couldn't believe it! The next day, the poor girl whose show I had taken, returned, packed up her belongings with much slamming and banging, interspersed with dirty looks in my direction. I have never seen her again, to this very day.

Across the street from the studio there was a speakeasy which contributed nothing but trouble to our operation. Knowing how I, a WCTU'er, felt about liquor and especially drinking on the job, it was the delight of some of the announcers to cover my desk every night with empty whiskey bottles.

These were the days of practical jokes on the air. One afternoon I was doing a show, playing the piano and "singing," when the door to the studio opened and in came three of the worst of the culprits, eating a slab of apple pie. They chewed on and on, in time to my every musical number. Another day, one of them hid under the piano, since I had previously locked the door to the studio, and just as I started the theme song, he grabbed my ankles and held on to them during the entire program. Every Saturday afternoon, I tightly belted my white trench coat, packed my make-up, and proceeded to the manager's office to quit. He always pretended that next week would be different and that the horseplay would stop. So I went on for three years. Sometimes I would have to start a program while the vocalist was sent for at the bar across the street. And one time I played an entire half-hour, for upon his arrival, he opened his mouth and fell down, dead drunk, carrying the microphone with him. These were trying times, indeed.

But there was a lot of fun also for us all. I played a program of double-piano with a sponsor's wife on the Fourth of July. While we were rendering a special arrangement of "Stars and Stripes Forever," in came three of the laughing boys, dressed like the Spirit of '76. They marched up and down the studio, and as we struck the final chord, one struck the point of the flag, which they were carrying, into the false ceiling, and left it hanging there. Their marching had set up such a flurry that the sponsor's wife's music blew away, and in her effort to retrieve it, all the hairpins from the bun of hair on her neck fell out. I had to play solo throughout the rest of the program. She dissolved into near hysterics and then and there renounced her musical career.

Another afternoon, while I was accompanying a bass singer who had chosen to do the "Volga Boatman," in came the same group, dragging a wooden casket by means of a tow-rope. The casket had been "borrowed" from a hotel storeroom where the Knights of Columbus kept their regalia. Seated in the casket was one of the boys, wearing a befrilled baby's cap, and the others were pulling him in perfect rhythm to the music—da, da da da, etc.

After the sponsor's wife "retired," Duane Snodgrass and I took over the program. But even then, the antics continued. He would carry on unbelievably at the piano, striking the final note of each arpeggio with his heel.

A game which we loved to play was called "Perfect Pitch." Duane would rush madly into the studio and hit a chord, which was most difficult to identify, on the piano. Then I had to rush in and play the same chord in the right key and with all the diminished and augmented notes in their right places. Then it would be my turn to try to stump him.

About this time, a miniature golf course was opened nearby. It was such a success with our boys that one day I had to run the controls for the records, do the announcements, and give the station breaks all afternoon. I will say the manager called them to task for this, but it didn't have too much effect, since he was one of the gang.

After about three years the Columbia Broadcasting System bought the station outright, and a far different atmosphere prevailed. They chose a very fine man, Timothy Goodman, as manager. However, radio was still a baby that seemed to thrive on turmoil. It was growing, to be sure, but it still needed guidance. Columbia fixed up the studios (they needed it) and we began to try to present programs that were of more intellectual character and prestige. By this time I had developed the "Woman's Hour," wherein we interviewed many guests from all possible fields. On looking back into my guest books, I find many names of college professors, lawyers, people from the entertainment world, sports people, and especially people from foreign countries—the governor of Hawaii, who wrote, "Ruth Lyons makes words into music," ambassadors from India, Germany, Holland,

France, Canada, China, and just about everywhere. It seems to me on looking back, that the entire world was traveling to America during these prewar years. We also depended on the Cincinnati Summer Opera for many of our guests, who were lured to perform on the program by Bernice Foley. I find among the names those of Giovanni Martinelli, Coe Glade, Gladys Swarthout, James Melton, Vivienne della Chiesa, along with many others.

Mr. H. V. Kaltenborn came to Cincinnati, and developed an ailment which hospitalized him, but he insisted on doing his evening programs from his hospital room, and I produced them all. I also produced a broadcast each Saturday morning to the CBS network from the Cincinnati Conservatory of Music, featuring the orchestra. The first trumpeter in the orchestra was a student there, Al Hirt, and each Friday I produced the afternoon concerts of the Cincinnati Symphony Orchestra to CBS. Eugene Goossens was its marvelous conductor at that time. There was great difficulty at first in securing a good "pickup." We had microphones hung everywhere, but still the right blend was not achieved. Then I conceived the idea that in Music Hall, where the broadcast originated, the audience heard the orchestra as a unit, so why not broadcast it that way. I had the engineers hang one microphone just above the conductor's head. Mr. Goossens was furious at first, but I prevailed upon him to try it. At the end of the broadcast we received a call from New York, which said it was the finest broadcast to date and asking what pickup we had used. When we told them that it was done on the one microphone, they were amazed. But still all was not peace and quiet.

One day we were told that a famous singer's promotion man would arrive, and I was to set up auditions for her to select a winner to represent Cincinnati on her full network

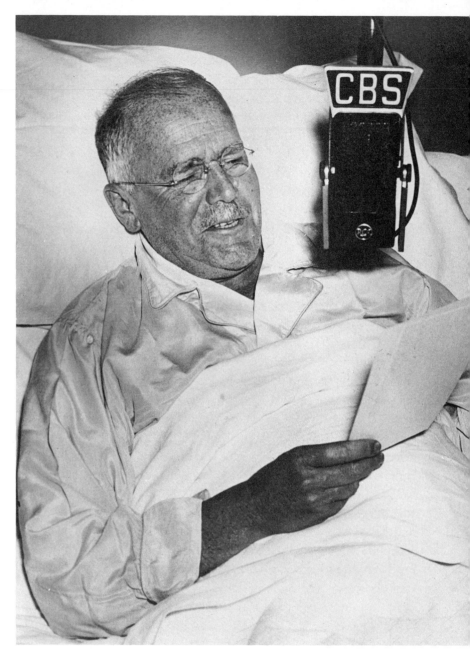

Mr. H. V. Kaltenborn, broadcasting from his hospital bed.

show, which would originate from the WKRC studios. I will never know the number of auditions I played. Everyone was becoming radio-minded, and everyone wanted to perform. After weeks of auditions, the promotion man arrived and narrowed the prospects to ten individuals. There were two or three that I thought had a chance to win, one an excellent pianist from the Conservatory of Music. But I was horrified when her manager insisted that we include a harmonica player. He said that she liked variety in the finals and that she would make the final choice. When she arrived we were all in a dither. Her personal manager took complete charge during that tense week, but she herself was very calm about it all. I, trying to be hospitable, took her to a place famous for its ice cream, and every day thereafter she sent for more of the same. She sat and listened to the finalists with a somewhat bored attitude, and, yes, she chose the harmonica player. We were completely stunned, but not for long. The evening papers carried a front-page picture and story about the contest winner. Almost immediately they received a call from a woman who said she was his ex-wife and that she had been trying everywhere to find him. He owed her alimony, and was also wanted to take care of his children.

The night of the broadcast, this famous person simply added another number to the program, and no one represented Cincinnati. And this, from a city that boasted a great Symphony Orchestra, the Summer Opera Company, the May Festival, and the home of the College of Music and the Conservatory of Music.

I have always admired this singer's beautiful voice, and I liked her personally, but I have never forgotten this incident of bored disinterest and the humiliation she caused us.

The Columbia Broadcasting System had decided to build

new studios and offices in the same Alms Hotel where they first started.

And then came the 1937 flood.

While we were building the new studios, we broadcast some of our programs from the Conservatory of Music. I shall never forget this period. I returned to the studio one Friday afternoon to find that the air was filled with bulletins of the imminence of a tremendous flood. It was raining very hard then, and we were all given rooms in the Alms Hotel so that we might be standing by, should we be needed. All day Saturday the rain continued to pour down. On Sunday, termed Black Sunday in Cincinnati, the situation worsened. Another girl and I were quartered on the twelfth floor of the hotel with no electricity, hence no elevator service, and only a bathtub filled in advance with cold water. We slept on desks in the studio from Sunday morning until Tuesday. During that time I did not leave the microphone. We had a direct line into City Hall, and constantly warned everyone to evacuate where the waters were coming up fast, to dispatch sandbags, to boil all drinking water, and to donate to the Red Cross. I shall never forget one man driving to the studio on that Black Sunday for more than one hundred miles to bring his contribution, a Mason jar filled with over ten dollars in change. We had a clothing drive also. In all, we raised sixty-five thousand dollars for the flood sufferers. On Tuesday afternoon a police officer took me downtown to see what I had been talking about for days. We got into a rowboat and rowed in the downtown streets over the tops of the street lights.

Into all this confusion came Floyd Gibbons, wearing high leather boots and followed by three secretaries, each equipped with a portable typewriter. His now historic broadcast to the nation everywhere was so highly exaggerated that people from New York, Chicago, and as far away as Los Angeles tied up the telephone lines completely, calling to see if their friends or relatives were still alive.

The broadcast was scheduled for Tuesday night. Our manager was given a script at 5 P.M., but what a shock when we heard Mr. Gibbons telling the nation that the water was rising around his ankles, and the screams of telephone operators were heard as they supposedly leaped from the windows. The next day the newspapers and radio stations did all they could to refute the broadcast. Later, Mr. Gibbons was subpoenaed by a New York court for false reporting, and we were all notified of the action. But nothing ever came of it.

On Thursday I made it home, only to see a man jump from a second-story window, miss the police boat below, and drown. These were dark days for Cincinnati, where millions of dollars of loss were incurred in the downtown business section and surrounding localities. As the water finally receded and the mopping-up jobs were completed, I discovered to my complete surprise that I had become the heroine of the inundation. I was then doing an hour-long morning show, plus another half-hour show called "A Woman Views the News," in addition to an afternoon musical show for the discovery of new talent. Suddenly, sponsors began to appear from everywhere. It seemed I had gained through a disaster, the confidence of the public. I had just done what was necessary in a crisis, but all sorts of awards from the mayor, the Red Cross, the police department, the city fire department, and most important of all, from the populace itself, came my way. And in order to take care of all the sponsors, I was asked to start an afternoon show of an hour's duration.

My father was quite ill again that summer, and my dear mother, in nursing him back to convalescence, completely exhausted herself. She died the next fall, the week before I was to begin my new show in the afternoon. This was my first experience with death, and I just couldn't quite accept it, but there was always that inexplicable little box called radio that needed to be fed incessantly, no matter what personal tragedy struck. And so I went on.

In the autumn of 1937 the station was purchased by the Taft Broadcasting Company. This meant another change in management, with young Hulbert Taft, Jr. in charge, under the direct supervision of his father, who was the editor of the *Times-Star* newspaper. And with the purchase by the Tafts, we were forced to find a new network. Everyone began to look for new jobs. We lost the boys who did our highly successful show, "The Dawn Patrol," and many others. And to add to our problems, AFTRA called a strike in order to unionize the station. There has never been a fairer or kindlier man than Hulbert Taft, Jr. But his father was of the old school, and having always had, and made money, he could not understand why this "fool radio station" wasn't doing the same thing.

We who remained tried even harder than ever to help the new management. We broadcast a show each Sunday morning to the Mutual Network, each week featuring a special guest, and I wrote a song every week for the show. When one of our guests was a famous orchestra leader, he wanted to buy five of them. However, he said they would have to be published under his name. I refused to agree to this, and I have never regretted it. We had as guests, people such as Benny Goodman, Ray Bolger, Charles "Buddy" Rogers, Henry Busse, the Andrews Sisters, the Boswell Sisters, Doris Day, Bernie Cummins, Guy Lombardo, Sammy Kaye, Laurel and Hardy, Jimmy Durante, Harry James, Eddy Duchin, José Iturbi, Jan Peerce, and Nelson Eddy, to mention a few.

Hulbert Taft, Jr.

Laurel and Hardy were our special guests this day.

And this was at eleven o'clock on Sunday morning.

When Ben Bernie was in town, I heard that he was looking for a boy vocalist. On our afternoon show, we had discovered a handsome young lad with a good baritone voice. The only problem was that he could not read music, and had to be taught everything by memory. However, one afternoon I went with him to try out for the job. Bernie did the tryouts from the stage of the Palace Theatre before an audience. I had to sit in the front row and nod my head each time our boy was to come in. He got the job and started to learn to read music, and he stayed with Bernie for quite some time. His name was Bob Allen. The last time I heard from him, he was in Hollywood.

One summer afternoon a group of us went to the Children's Hospital to put on a show for the little sick children there. I had never been in a children's hospital before, and although this one was a fine new building, I was shocked at the cold, sad interior, with no toys or pictures for these dear little children who were sick and away from their parents. It kept coming back to my mind. So a few weeks before Christmas I told my radio audience what was troubling me, especially when, after calling the hospital as to what was done at Christmastime for the children, I was told that each one received an orange and a little candy and that a small Christmas tree was set up in the lobby. I couldn't believe that this was true. So I begged my audience to send me a nickel, a dime, or whatever they could spare, and we would really make it Christmas for these little children in the hospital. The response was most gratifying, and we received one thousand dollars that first year. We went to the city's leading toy store and bought dolls, games, books, crayons, and trucks, and wrapped them all alone. Then on Christmas Eve we took them to the hospital, with one of our staff dressed as

Santa Claus. It made Christmas much more meaningful for each of us, and delighted the children and the hospital staff. Thus, on the Eve of Christmas, 1939, the Ruth Lyons' Christmas Fund began!

Because of my father's adamant Republicanism, and since I was working for a station owned by the cousin of Mr. Republican himself, Robert A. Taft, I went in 1940 to the big rally and parade in Elwood, Indiana for Wendell Willkie. However, by the time of FDR's third inauguration, realizing that this was an unprecedented historical occasion, I went to Washington for President Roosevelt's inaugural parade and ball. I loved Robert A. Taft and his lovely wife Martha. But somehow in the hotel I met up with Mr. Charles Sawyer, a good Democrat, later Ambassador to Belgium and then Secretary of Commerce. And under his guidance I didn't miss a thing at the inauguration. I consider Mr. Sawyer one of the most astute and kindly men I have ever known. I went from Washington to New York, where I sold two of my songs, "Let's Light the Christmas Tree," which I had written to aid in raising the Ruth Lyons' Christmas Fund, and "Fooled."

When I returned, my father was ill again, and my many shows were becoming increasingly difficult for me to do day after day. I considered giving up my work on the air and devoting my energy to being program and music director only. But something my mother once said to me, when I had mentioned doing this very thing came back to me, and it was this, "As long as the public accepts you and you bring pleasure to them, stay right where you are. No one can take your good name away from you, but those behind the scenes are often replaced."

So my sister and I took an apartment, sold all my mother's fine glassware and china, never realizing their true worth,

Here I am in 1940, with WKRC.

and prepared for a simpler way of life. My father suffered another stroke and never saw the new apartment, as for two and a half years he was in the hospital and in a rest home.

On December 7, 1941, I was driving with Cliff Lash, who later became the pianist on my WLW show, to Music Hall to see a ballet, when the news of Pearl Harbor was flashed on the radio. I must confess it didn't mean too much to me at first, and I could not imagine why the editor of the *Cincinnati Enquirer,* our morning paper, rushed wildly out of the door when we told him about it in the foyer of Music Hall. But reality came later, when the President spoke that night over radio and when, just a few months later, one of the boys in our studio band left for the Army.

That spring most of my interviews were with Army colonels, Navy officers, food specialists, and other people involved in the war effort. We played golf almost daily at California Public Links, getting up at seven o'clock to be on the first tee at seven-thirty, and then to work. I had been studying at the University of Cincinnati and had won a scholarship to study piano at the College of Music. My expenses, due to my father's illness, were enormous. I did manage to buy a gray Chrysler convertible that lasted out the war. Then one day I received a call from WLW. I paid no attention to it, thinking that it was in regard to a joint Community Chest program we were planning in connection with them. However, the program director called again and said it was urgent that I come to see James Shouse and Bob Dunville. I finally went, and they offered me a job on WLW and WSAI, which Crosley then also owned.

I had to tell Mr. Taft that after thirteen years I was leaving to work for the opposition, and to make it worse, I had to go to his home where he was recovering from a broken leg. WKRC had just been named the most progressive station in Cincinnati in a poll taken by *Variety* magazine. My "Woman's Hour" program rated higher than any program on WLW. And the station won in nearly every category. Mr. Taft was his usual kindly self, and said that he understood perfectly. WKRC was a 15,000 watt station compared to WLW, which was 150,000 watts. And he proved his great friendship for me and for what he said I had done for him many years later, when he gave a dinner for me to view the new WKRC television studios the night before the official opening. As he took me through the magnificent studios and pointed out the electronically controlled systems, I turned to him and asked, "But where are the color cameras?" In all seriousness he asked, "Do you really think color will be important?"

When Hulbert Taft, Jr. was killed in an explosion recently, the radio and television industry and Cincinnati in general lost a truly fine gentleman and civic leader. But I lost a true friend.

chapter five

I Move to WLW

▪▪

During that spring while I was completing my remaining time at WKRC, I attended a concert at Music Hall. Lily Pons was the soloist. Seated in front of me was a very handsome young man, who looked quite familiar. During the intermission, he turned around and asked if I would like to walk around a bit. As we were going up the aisle, he told me his name was Herman Newman and that we had met before at the University of Cincinnati. I remembered him then, and asked him what he had been doing since school days. What hadn't he been doing might have been a better question. He had graduated from the University of Cincinnati, spent a year in law school, studied in Chicago for the Unitarian ministry, had won a scholarship to Oxford, England, had traveled through Europe, filled a pulpit in Erie, Pennsylvania, for six years, and then had come back to Cincinnati, and was at that time, doing social work. He had dark hair, blue eyes, and a beautiful deep voice.

I had my first date with him the following weekend, and "it was love at first sight." On that first date he brought me a quart of wild strawberries, and ever since I have collected dishes, ornaments, and other treasured items, all bearing this decoration. We discussed everything, including my making the change to WLW. He suggested that I at least try it—and he also suggested that I marry him immediately. But I told him of my father's critical illness and that I could not ask him to share that financial burden. You see, my father had suffered great losses in the stock market during the Great Depression, and I was sole support at that time of my father and younger sister Rose. The radio industry did not suffer much from the Depression. It was business as usual.

So on July 6, 1942, I started working for WLW and WSAI, both owned by Powell Crosley, Jr. I took with me from WKRC fourteen sponsors who were scheduled to be on the WSAI show. As an added inducement, WLW offered me a fifteen-minute show every morning, which bore the impressive name of "The Consumer's Foundation." This show used the services of two hundred women, who were asked from time to time to test the products to be advertised on the show. My reception at WLW was anything but cordial by many of the staff, especially the girls, with the exception of the engineering staff. They were impressed because the engineers at WKRC had sent me a basket of flowers for my first broadcast. Engineers I have always found to be a fine breed of humans, and they do stick together.

I started out getting my listeners to enter a contest for a name for my WSAI show. I have always been of the opinion that the listeners should participate in every way possible, to engender the success of a show. The name "Petticoat Party Line" was chosen. I was to have a band on the show, and was to have free rein in doing my commercials.

At WLW, things were not as uncomplicated as they had been at WKRC. It was a much larger organization in every way. And it took me a few months to learn who all the people were and what their jobs were.

The publicity director had conceived a contest to interest people in buying War Bonds. A popular announcer who had his own show was to vie with me, and whoever sold the most War Bonds would be named "Mayor of Cincinnati" for a day. The contest was to end on a certain Saturday at 5 P.M. We both worked very hard. I felt that I had a great deal at stake as far as my future was concerned at WLW, that I was "put on the spot," so to speak.

The early part of the week that the contest was to end, my father died. His funeral was held on Thursday. The next morning I returned to work, to find my secretary sobbing bitterly. It so happened that on the day of my father's funeral, a large rally had been held in one of the suburbs, and my opponent, who was in attendance, had counted in his total all the bonds sold. I was beaten by about ten thousand dollars' worth of bond sales. The tears of that secretary of mine and the injustice she felt had been done to me, compelled me to action. Saturday morning bright and early I began making calls on many of my old friends that I had met in the business world, literally begging them to buy bonds. The gentleman who had been manager of WKRC was first on my list of prospects. He bought five thousand dollars' worth, and suggested several of his friends, even phoning them and making appointments for me to see them. After six such calls, I had sold thirty thousand dollars' worth of War Bonds, but I wanted to make this a decisive victory. My last call was on Leonard Minster, then the head of Shillito's large department store in Cincinnati. He purchased ten thousand dollars' worth of bonds from me. Is it any wonder that this magnificent store has always been a favorite of mine?

I had not told anyone at the studio what I was going to do. I got back to WLW at quarter of five in the afternoon. My loyal secretary was still in tears. But not for long. I winked at her, and at five o'clock exactly I walked into the publicity office and presented the forty thousand dollars' worth of bonds to the publicity director. I had won the contest fair and square (and with a great deal of leg work), and the following Monday I was named "Mayor for a Day" by His Honor, Mayor James Garfield Stewart, whose son is now Justice Potter Stewart of the Supreme Court. From that day on, Mayor Stewart, who was elected six times as Mayor of Cincinnati, appeared every New Year's Day as a guest on my program. No matter how late he had been out to celebrate the coming of the new year, he always appeared, fresh-shaven and immaculately dressed, while the studio band played his favorite number, "When My Dreamboat Comes Home."

Herman and I were married on October 3, 1942, in a Presbyterian minister's home. We honeymooned at charming Beaumont Inn in Kentucky. On the way home Herman was driving, and all along the road were stands where bunches of bittersweet were being sold. He stopped the car a little way past one stand and got out to get me a bunch. I, trying to be helpful, slid over into the driver's seat and started to back the car to where he was standing. Just then he started toward the car, and it grazed his leg. He has accused me ever since of trying to get rid of him on our honeymoon.

We started out in our new home very happy. But the first spring of our marriage Herman came home with a case of scarlet fever, contracted on his rounds as a Juvenile Court worker. We were quarantined. I shall never forget the excitement this caused. The telephone company put lines into the house, and each day an engineer was sent out from the studio to arrange for the broadcast. One in particular (Walt Rogers) was scared to death of the disease, and he would sit outside

Mayor Stewart, who appeared every New Year's Day on my program.

WSAI engineer Walt Rogers, doing the broadcast from our home during quarantine.

Guy Lombardo visits with me over WSAI.

every day and hand the mike, with a long cord on it, in through the window. Luckily, it was a warm spring that year.

I was supposed to write the morning show on WLW, and read it on the air. I did this for about a week and was never more miserable. Then I just started to ad-lib it with the announcer, thereby breaking one of the cardinal rules of the "Nation's Station." My first announcer was George Skinner, now an executive at CBS in New York. He was followed by Jay Stewart, at present seen daily on the popular ABC show "Let's Make a Deal."

For months all went well, until one day, immediately after the show I received a call from the vice-president of WLW, Robert Dunville, to come to his office and bring the script from that morning's program. My knees quaking, I went to his office and confessed that I had not been writing the show for months, but had been ad-libbing it. I fully expected a real blowup, but Mr. Dunville laughed and said he knew that I had been working without script and he thought that it was time to let me work in my own way on WLW, as I had been doing all along on WSAI. And then and there was born the "Morning Matinee."

A big band was added to the show, and I chose as my co-worker a young man from Rushville, Indiana, Frazier Thomas. Frazier was a natural for the assignment, and it was great fun to work with him. When I came to WLW, I was encouraged to continue the Ruth Lyons' Christmas Fund. So when "Morning Matinee" came into being, we started the fund in 1943 and raised fifty-four thousand dollars that year. Of course, with the added coverage we had on WLW, the fund started to grow. We expanded its use to a hospital in Indiana, one in Louisville, Kentucky, as well as the Children's Hospital in Cincinnati. The show began to attract new sponsors immediately. Since it was a new concept in radio, many sponsors tried to buy short-term contracts, and this caused my first real differences with the sales department. I felt that to make advertising honest, I should try to take a personal approach in talking about the products I presented. The sales manager thought otherwise. He tried to persuade me to advertise one brand of coffee one week, and another the next. The management finally agreed that I had a sound idea, but what skirmishes we had. For instance, while I was on my first vacation, one company had purchased a large order of pins, or as they called them, "exact replicas of an old Victorian brooch." They had brought some of them to the studio, and my boss had agreed that I would offer them to the listeners for a proof of purchase of their product. When I returned from vacation, I took one look at the pins and saw that they were simply pressed out of gilded tin. I refused point-blank to describe them in glowing terms or to offer them to my listeners. I was accused of insubordination, of embarrassing the station, and affronting the sponsor. But I knew that all I was doing was trying to be honest with my audience. The argument raged on, pro and con, and then I had an idea. The two hundred women who still were listed in the "Consumer's Foundation" could help me. We sent one of the pins to each one of them with the sponsor's description, and we asked them if they considered that the product lived up to the advertising. The answer was an overwhelming, "No!" And so I won the first in a long list of confrontations with both management and sponsors.

There was a very amusing aftermath to the pin episode. Several years later, I was invited to New York to meet our sales people there. We had a lovely luncheon at one of the hotels. Everyone made speeches and was introduced, and at the end of the luncheon our New York sales manager rose and said that in appreciation for my cooperation and help in making their sales soar, they wished to present me with a token of their esteem. They handed me a beautifully wrapped box. With great anticipation I opened it and noted that it bore the name "Tiffany" on the top. However, nestling in the white satin lining, was one of those dreadful tin pins.

But business was booming. Every morning bus loads of people arrived at the studio coming from all over our listening area, to "see" our radio show, "Morning Matinee." One morning there were ten bus loads, and the people had to be seated in our two studios, one on the second floor, and one on the fifth. We did the show racing up and down by grace of the kindly elevator.

The year 1944 was one never to be forgotten. On August 27, 1944, at 7:34 in the morning, our dearly beloved Candace Laird Newman was born. We called her Candy. Several weeks after Candy's birth, I broadcast from home, and daughter made her debut at the mike at the age of six weeks. Our house was filled once more with the comings and goings of engineers, and that Christmas, the Ruth Lyons' Christmas Fund swelled to one hundred thousand dollars.

These were the years of World War II, and I was engaged in numerous activities for the USO and other activities for the boys overseas. I did a series of broadcasts to Great Britain telling the British housewives about conditions in America. These were aired on the BBC, and in return I used many tapes made by them featuring Mrs. Rose Buckner, who told us about the many problems they were having in Britain at that time. My greatest problem was in securing ration stamps for gasoline and especially for shoes. Many of my listeners sent me their shoe stamps, for which I was very grateful.

During 1945 the "Morning Matinee" pursued a very successful course. We did original singing commercials, programs in costume, and we enrolled over eighty thousand

One of our wonderful "Morning Matinee" audiences.

children under twelve years of age in our birthday roster. Each child was sent a birthday card bearing a picture of one of the features of the show, The Peppermint Horse. This was a wooden horse from an old merry-go-round which we had painted with red and white stripes and mounted on a platform, in the studio. Every morning each child who attended the show had a make-believe ride on that horse. I can't begin to enumerate the number of young mothers who in later years came to my shows and proudly showed me their birthday cards they had received when they were children. We had a margarine sponsor for whom I wrote a singing jingle. Each morning the children were invited on stage to sing it. The one who sang the loudest was awarded a silver dollar. I can never forget those little souls, straining their vocal cords, particularly one little boy, whose face I noticed was very red and broke out in big blotches as he sang. When I commented on this, his mother explained that their other two children, whom she had left at home, had the measles. I often wondered how far that epidemic spread!

About this time the Avco Corporation bought WLW, and WSAI was also sold. We had to start a new show on WLW in addition to the "Morning Matinee." We had sponsors waiting in line to participate. It had occurred to me that there were thousands of women from nearby small towns who had never had luncheon in a big hotel. After negotiating with the Gibson Hotel, we arranged to do a broadcast from there, after lunch. But what about the cost of the lunch? With great fear and trepidation I told my audience about the new show we had in mind, and invited them to send in for tickets. The tickets cost one dollar per person. The next morning we were deluged with mail, and we had sold enough tickets for the next three years. We called the show the "Fifty Club," as there were tickets sold to fifty ladies a day. The hotel built a special room on the mezzanine floor, where the luncheon was served and the broadcast originated. There was no band; I played the show's theme song on a small piano! We had a few prizes daily, especially a coveted hat modeled by my announcer, Paul Jones, who was the announcer at this time on the "Fifty Club." We gave household hints and played musical chairs, with a prize to the woman who finally wound up on the magic chair. What a scramble! We had guests from the theatre, writers, and others of note who came to town, and the women loved it. And this is the manner in which the "Fifty Club" was born. I was urged by the management to call the show the "Ruth Lyons' Luncheon Show," but I have never used my name in connection with any show that I have done, for I always felt that should I leave the show, it might well continue without my name.

These were wonderful days. We did the morning show at the studio, and then went down to the hotel. What fun we had each day! My two secretaries, Elsa Sule and Suzi King, and I picked out the hats to be given each day, and enjoyed our work immensely. The "Fifty Club" was sponsored by Procter & Gamble. "Morning Matinee" was sold out. So it seemed to me to be the propitious time to take the show on the road. We chose to do a show in Muncie, Indiana. It was a long trip, and it snowed very hard that Friday morning. But the crowd that turned out to greet us filled the theatre with standing room only. We also decided to go to Louisville and to Indianapolis as well as the hospital in Cincinnati to put on a show for the children in the hospitals which were then a part of the Christmas Fund. The morning of our visit to Indianapolis, I woke up about four o'clock and discovered my entire body was broken out in immense hives. The doctor came and gave me a shot of adrenalin, and very shaken and scared, I caught the train to Indiana. This was just a week before Christmas, and many soldiers and sailors were traveling on holiday leave. I had gained quite a bit of weight, due to the delicious pies and cakes served at the hotel where the "Fifty Club" originated, and I was in terrible misery, from my girdle. But at the Riley Memorial Hospital I forgot temporarily my own discomfort, when a little blind boy, just four years old, insisted that I, and I alone, give him a tool chest and let him feel each tool. At all the Christmas parties we had a crying room, where we would go before the parties and weep as they brought the little stricken ones in wheelchairs and carts to the various playrooms. We almost didn't get home that day, as the trains were overcrowded and the boys in uniform, deservedly so, were allowed to board them first. We stood in line for six hours before we could get on a train for Cincinnati. I shall never forget Frazier Thomas, who was the announcer on the "Morning Matinee," following me through car after car of boys in uniform, muttering loudly, "If I had known your mother was going to send us coach tickets, I wouldn't have come home for Christmas." When I finally reached home at one o'clock, Herman had to cut my girdle off. I had the hives for six weeks, which afforded me a well-earned vacation.

When I returned to work, it was necessary for us to have another ticket sale. This time we sold tickets for four years. And so began the seventh year of the "Fifty Club" on radio.

chapter six

Early Television

•••

WLW had been experimenting with television since 1937. In 1948 the first commercial program was presented. At home we had a small seven-inch set, but I paid very little attention to it, except to watch an occasional basketball game. Herman and Candy had bought the set, and both were greatly intrigued by it. It was fun to watch those early shows on television. There was a show on Sunday afternoon which was telecast from our Cincinnati Zoo which was the beginning of Candy's interest in Japanese spaniels. Later we acquired eight of these lovable little dogs.

In 1949 I was told that the "Fifty Club" was to go on television. This was a terrible blow to me! I was too fat, and television added at least ten pounds to one's appearance. I finally agreed to try it for one week. This was in May 1949. WLW had built a large building high on one of Cincinnati's many hills, which meant that we had to leave the Gibson Hotel and hire a caterer to provide the luncheon for the women. And most disappointing of all, our sponsor for the past five years, Procter & Gamble, refused to continue sponsoring the show. When I think of the use P & G has made of television during the ensuing years, this seems impossible to understand. Years later, they were one of our dominant sponsors.

I shall never forget that first week on television. It was pure torture. In those days, the engineers were in complete control of everything connected with television. One even wore a beret! I arrived at the studio the first morning to find the women sitting at the tables with all the hot lights in the studio beating down on them, and it was a very warm day to begin with. I started to remonstrate at once, and as I crossed the studio, a voice came from out of nowhere, "Miss Lyons, the first rule of television is never to cross in front of a camera." I hadn't even seen the cameras! Then the boys began to tell me where I must stand, sit, where I should be when talking with the women in the audience, and that I must always face the camera. While on radio, I had been accustomed to moving about a great deal while doing the show. It seemed as though those comfortable days were gone forever.

At the end of that first week, I marched into Mr. Dunville's office and told him I wanted no part of television and that I had done my last show that day. I recall his reply to the effect that television was here to stay and would be around for a long time after I was gone. How right he was! Not until September, however, did I return to television. All during that summer I worked very hard. I was made program director of WLW-TV, and I learned much about the new medium from the ground up. The first thing I did was to cut down on the lighting. We were the very first to use cool incandescent lights. I made trips to Chicago and New York, where I attended a rehearsal of the "Perry Como Show." Sitting in the audience, I saw nothing but a line of cameras across the stage. I made up my mind right then and there that I would never work with cameras between me and my studio audience.

And to this day this pattern has continued. Another thing that upset me was that I wanted to see what the viewing audience saw. I finally convinced the engineers to place a monitor just off the set, so that I could watch the show as I did it. The boys kept saying that this would cause a feedback, but I didn't want to hear, just merely see what was going on. So during that long summer I worked at least fourteen hours a day, and I lost forty pounds, which I have never regained. My former secretary, Vera Tyson, who had been with me at WKRC, came to WLW, and she was indeed a great help to me. We created a full daytime schedule, in addition to the "Fifty Club." Among our first staff additions were Bill Nimmo, Betty Clooney, and many more. I was supposed to keep the job as program director for six months, but it continued on for nine months. In October, John T. Murphy, now president of Avco Corporation, was brought in from Dayton, Ohio, as manager of WLW-TV. And a few months after his arrival, the co-axial cable joined us to NBC-TV. Finally we were well on our way.

A funny thing occurred during those days. The engineers finally agreed that I might have a set where I could view what we were doing. And it was the most decrepit old set in existence. I'm sure Noah must have used it on the Ark. The picture was fuzzy, and kept rolling constantly. In vain I tried to get the Crosley Company, which then was manufacturing sets, to send me a new model, but to no avail. So one day on the show, I said that if any dealer who sold TV sets would send one to me, I would have it set up and would mention his name. The next morning as I drove up the hill to the TV studios, I almost didn't make the show. There was a long line of trucks, lined up to the very door, and inside were nineteen television sets being installed. I was so delighted that I gave each one of them a "plug." The next day they were moved

Mr. John T. Murphy.

Our "Fifty-Fifty" Club audience waits to get into the show.

out by order of the management, and a brand new Crosley set was finally installed. Sometimes you have to resort to drastic means in order to achieve a very simple thing.

We did the "Fifty Club" for over a year on the hill, and then WLW purchased the Elks Theatre at Ninth and Elm Streets, and all television operations were moved downtown once more. It was time for another ticket sale and the demand for tickets was so great that we sold them for the next three years, and increased the number of women daily in our studio audience to one hundred. And it was then that we adopted the name "Fifty-Fifty Club." One large studio on the second floor was converted into a kitchen and dining room, where the luncheon was served, and the television studio was located on the fifth floor. I hired extra girls to handle the ticket sale, several of whom remained with me to take care of that year's Christmas Fund and to handle the ever-increasing daily mail.

Everything possible happened during those early television days. Everyone was constantly on edge. One boy, when it was time for him to go on, lost his nerve and froze completely. Another, when I finally found him, was in his office sitting cross-legged on top of his desk, crying hysterically.

On our return to the downtown studios, we began to concentrate on bringing more guests to meet our audiences. I thoroughly enjoyed these interviews and the many lovely people that I met. And about the same time sponsors began to realize the value of television. Our first producer of the "Fifty Club" was a young man named Gene Walz, who has lately returned to Cincinnati, plus four young sons, as a public relations man for a competitive station.

One noontime I was walking around the audience, chatting with the women, when I heard my name called very clearly. I turned around and asked who it was in the audience who had called to me. No one had said a word. Immediately following the program I received a call from New York. A former manager of one of Cincinnati's theatres was calling to tell me an incredible story. His wife was extremely ill, and had not spoken a word in more than a year. In trying to interest her in just about anything, he had purchased a small television set and placed it in her bedroom. At first she paid no attention to it at all, but on this particular day, when I was so sure that I heard someone speak my name, he had turned the set on again for her. Suddenly, she sat up in bed and said, "Ruth Lyons." She had been a faithful listener to me on radio for several years before going to New York. Her husband was jubilant. This was a genuine example of ESP. Later, she wrote to me to tell me of her complete recovery.

Another day while the show was in progress, I noticed a woman sitting in the front row suddenly slump over in her seat. I moved to the other side of the studio so that the cameras would not show her while they brought a stretcher and carried her out. The show went on, but the dear woman was dead. This was a dreadful experience.

But all was not tragedy. Those first days of television were like reliving the first days of radio all over again. Many weird and funny things happened. We had a boy vocalist on the show, who was quite a favorite with the women. He had, however, a strange habit of taking away the things we had as prizes. Each day we were given a beautiful flower arrangement from a local florist. Day after day when the time came for the show, the flowers were nowhere to be found. I called the florist several times, and he always said they had been delivered that morning. One day, our lad grew a bit careless. I had noticed that he always left the studio immediately after the show. And on this particular day I saw that he was carrying something under his coat. I ran after him, and chased him for quite a distance. And sure enough, he had the flowers, beautifully arranged in a Chinese vase. When confronted with the fact that he had been taking the flowers day after day, he said that his mother loved flowers. Needless to say, his mother's daily floral offering from her devoted son ceased.

We played charades, and all of the girls in my office were participants. It was at this time that the question of heavy TV make-up arose. A girl was hired to teach us all how to use the make-up. I was not very popular with her. She insisted on a very heavy dark brown make-up, with dark brown lipstick, that looked as if I had just eaten a handful of chocolates, the kind that melt in your mouth, not in your hand. All this was made more ridiculous by covering with white make-up any laugh lines or wrinkles in the face. I simply refused to submit. I could not appear before a live audience made up to look like Minnehaha, but the other girls found something exciting about all this and ran about looking like a band of squaws for weeks. As one of my girls, who conformed in every way, said to me just the other day, she doesn't believe she has quite bleached out yet. I finally explained to the women in the audience all about this, and insisted that the girl who was doing the make-up come on the show and make me up in front of the camera. The howls of laughter proved that this was not for me.

Despite my bare face showing, the sponsors began to take over the show, and the show was lengthened to an hour and a half. I worked very hard to try to keep it interesting. I had as many as twenty sponsors a day, five days a week. We had a vocalist every day and a fine band under the direction of Cliff Lash, with whom I had worked at WKRC. We also had whatever prominent guests came to town or were performing in and around our area.

About this time the NBC network offered me a seven-year contract, to originate the show from Cincinnati to the network. We started out our first hour of the show fed to NBC, and then we had to do the last hour of it locally. The NBC portion was divided into quarter hours, with a break each quarter hour. In Chicago we opened the NBC station's telecasting for the day, and in New York, due to daylight saving time, we were seen at one o'clock instead of our regular noon hour. However, despite all these problems, we began to hear from people far and near. Most of the mail we received came from Atlanta, Georgia, and Boston, Massachusetts. And I began to realize that people were just the same everywhere in their response to the show. All of our time segments were sold. It was a great strain, however, since we were constantly being asked to check with New York as to what we were going to do each day. I didn't know what I was going to do, and I felt that much of the spontaneity of the show was being lost.

And then I went on a short vacation. When I returned, I found that several of our network sponsors were gone, and it was not until I received a telephone call from a good friend of mine in a New York agency that I realized what was happening. NBC was doing an afternoon show from New York, starring Kate Smith, and the order had been given to sell her show in preference to mine. Well, that did it! I came back to the studio before my vacation was over, and told our local salesmen that I was not going to continue with the network and that I wanted them to sell out the show locally by the time I returned to work. You see, we had to drop many local sponsors when we went on the network. Our boys did a tremendous job, and orders came flooding in. In fact, they were a bit overzealous, for we had to lengthen the show to two hours. The station backed me on my decision, for as always, money is the most vital factor involved in any commercial venture.

The two-hour stint was just too much for me to continue, however, and we cut back to one hour and a half. From that day on until I retired at the end of January 1967, the "Fifty-Fifty Club" remained a very remunerative and rewarding experience. And I was permitted to do the show the way I liked to do it, with the commercials integrated with songs, music, exposure of new talent, and the interviewing of guests, many of whom have remained my good friends throughout the years.

I have a theory about doing commercials. You cannot fool the viewers at any time. That television screen reveals your every thought. It proves conclusively whether you are genuinely interested in what you are selling and whether you are honest about your sponsors' products. This entails knowing the products and their saleability. I have had many an argument with salesmen, advertising agencies, and even with the sponsors themselves. If I didn't think I could sell a product, I turned it down. I have never underestimated the intelligence of the American housewife. I always assumed that she was much smarter than I in many ways, and much kinder too. One time when one of my housekeepers was ill, I brought Herman's shirts to the studio, set up six ironing boards with irons, and had the women compete to see who could iron a shirt in the quickest time. It so happened that one of our sponsor's products was a spray-on starch, which made it very convenient to work in the commercial. We had fun with some of the commercials, but they were all reputable products that lived up to their advertising claims. Mr. Bill McCluskey was our liaison man between the show and the sponsors, and he was of invaluable assistance to me in this job. The biggest problem was with products that had national distribution and who used taped commercials in other markets. But the sponsors soon learned that on our type of show, the way in which we wove the commercials into the whole show, between topics of interest, music, and guests, had a place in their over-all advertising. And so we persevered, until we had a long waiting list of sponsors, some of whom waited for several years to get on the show. I greatly prize a letter from a little boy, ten years old, that I received when I was doing twenty commercials a day. It read as follows: "Dear Miss Lyons, I love to watch your show, because it doesn't have any commercials." What higher tribute?

My first announcer was Paul Jones, a fine athlete who now works for a competitive station as a sportscaster. Then came a very funny man, Willie Thall. When he started on the show he was married and had two children, but his first wife died quite suddenly one Saturday morning, and we all mourned for him and his two small children. About a year later he remarried a widow with four small children of her own. Willie was a delight on television. He had a quick wit and could portray most realistically, with a very woebegone expression, the experiences of trying to adjust to the large family he had now acquired.

Willie was losing his hair and was the first of our group to buy a hairpiece. He flew to Cleveland one weekend to acquire the services of a specialist in that field. The first day he appeared on the show wearing it he took a terrible ribbing from the boys in the band, the set-up boys, and all of us. I shall never forget him telling about the night he went to a baseball game. It was a very hot night, and after trying for several hours to get his hairpiece on straight with the spirit gum he used, he finally decided to go without it. He wore a straw hat and was determined to keep it on all during the game, since much of the spirit gum still remained on his head.

After getting seated, he quickly went out behind the stands on the pretext of buying his son a hot dog, and remained there until after the playing of "The Star-Spangled Banner." Then, feeling that it was safe to keep his hat on for the rest of the game, he returned to his seat. But that was not the end of it. For as soon as the game started, a patron seated behind him leaned forward and touched him on the shoulder, asking him would he mind removing his hat, as it was interfering with her view of the game. With that he gave up, and dragging his protesting son, went home.

Willie stayed with me for about five jubilant years. We laughed constantly at his various antics—like the time he was holding the can of whipped cream, and due to the hot lights, it exploded all over him. The sponsor called and said he wished Willie would do this every time that his product was shown, and even offered to have Willie's suit cleaned each time.

And there was the day I asked Willie to drive me to a car showroom so that I might pick up my brand new car. I had a good friend who baked me a grape pie each fall, and I had received one that day at the studio. So I carried it with me when I went to pick up the car, intending to drive my new convertible home. But this was not to be! Willie was greatly intrigued by the new white and red upholstery and climbed into the back seat to admire it. Yes—you're right, the grape pie was on the back seat just where I had put it. So we had to leave the car to be cleaned up, and an abject Willie drove me home.

Willie would be panic-stricken whenever I went on vacation and he had to run the show with the help of the other members of the cast. So I was truly surprised when suddenly he left to head up his own show on another station in company with his wife. I am sorry to say, it didn't last long. He was greatly loved by our audience, and his name was mentioned with fondness long after he had left the "Fifty-Fifty Club." Since WLW has always had the policy of never letting anyone remain on the air once that person had given any indication of leaving, I was left in quite a quandary. First of all, I called Connie Boswell, who flew in from New York and did a great job of substitution. Then Frank Parker came to be on the show for two weeks, as did my good friend Dick Noel, from "Don McNeil's Breakfast Club." Dick had been a vocalist on our show during the days of radio. After that I began to audition, for a week at a time, many announcers at WLW and from other places also. Some of them were Jack Norwine, Sid Doherty, Johnny Reynolds, and Bob Braun. I did not want to replace Willie too soon, for I felt that in the minds of our viewers he was still very much a part of the show. And I decided then and there that I would never again depend on one announcer only. So early in 1957 I chose Bob Braun, who had recently joined the staff of WLW, and Peter Grant, our chief newscaster. Bob was a young man who was a winner on the "Arthur Godfrey Talent Scout" show. He was married and had a small son. Peter, on the other hand, had been at WLW for many years doing the eleven o'clock news. At first he was most reluctant to take on the job as co-host with me. He was, and still is a bachelor, despite my constant efforts to find a wife for him. He is a great gentleman, well informed, who, when he finally lost his temerity, even reached the point where we had him taking part in every facet of the show. We even got him to sing and dance. Having the two announcers on the show, each one different in his approach and appeal, gave me a wider scope in all the shows that were to come.

Our "Fifty-Fifty Club" audience was composed of intelligent and well-informed people—and the people who attended the show daily differed widely from those in the typical New York or Hollywood studio audience. There were no "regulars." The ticket situation prevented this. The men and women and children who came to Crosley Square for the noontime luncheon were well dressed and poised when they were in front of the cameras and microphones. The studio audience was a real part of the show. They entered into discussions with me freely—they offered suggestions, participated in commercials, and on occasion, ran the show.

Our audience at home was also well informed and intelligent—a fact attested to by the many splendid letters that came to the "Lyons' Den" each day. It was an audience composed not only of housewives, but of men, teen-agers, and children as well. While he was living, the noted author, Louis Bromfield, was a regular listener to the "Fifty-Fifty Club" and wrote to me frequently. Letters came not only from new brides seeking household hints, but from doctors and salesmen who listened to the program on their car radios, and from secretaries and office girls who turned on the show during their lunch hours. And many a boss was forced to buy a television set to keep the girls happy while the "Fifty-Fifty Club" was on. Also, youngsters coming home from school for lunch made up a great part of our audience. Whenever a member of the "Fifty-Fifty Club" cast went shopping, there were many questions to be answered from the sales people, who could watch only on their days off. The questions ranged form, "What guest will be on next Friday? The girl in the millinery department is off on Friday."—to "How did the story that Miss Lyons started last Tuesday and didn't finish, end?" The growing "Fifty-Fifty Club" audience was alive and alert, and I did my best to try to make them think about everything that was going on.

We strived constantly to give the show a new look. One

that I shall always remember with great enjoyment was a strange desk that was built for me to use daily on the show. It was simply huge, painted beige, and in the top of it was a trap door, from which a set-up boy underneath handed up the products as I talked about them. Eventually the boys cut a window in the front of it, fitted with glass. Underneath, the set-up boy, Ronnie Wilson, had outfitted for himself a very comfortable domain, complete with an electric fan, a small hot plate, an old quilt, several pillows, a small reading lamp, and all of the products on the show. He would wave through the window to the studio audience and sometimes hold up cards for them to read, as well as old pictures of me.

One day Ted Mack was my guest on the show. He was sitting next to me, when he suddenly grabbed me by the arm and fearfully whispered, "There's a man under this desk!"

Ronnie weighed over two hundred pounds, and his sense of humor was commensurate. He is now program director of WCET, the educational television station in Cincinnati, which now occupies the same building WLW had built up on the hill for their first telecast.

We had the McGuire Sisters as guests, Tommy Dorsey, Red Nichols, Margaret Whiting, Jack Teagarden, Dr. Walter Alvarez; the president of the AMA, Dr. Edward Annis; and Charles Goren, who brought me his latest book on bridge, which all of us in the office swore by. And what a great show we had when Gene Krupa came and played for us. Sal Mineo came also on the same day, as they were promoting the movie of Krupa's life story. Our drummer almost gave up his profession at that time.

When Roy Rogers and Dale Evans visited the show, it was necessary to bring Trigger up to the studio on the regular elevator. And who will ever forget Willie, who appeared in a streetcleaner's costume on that day, and luckily so.

chapter seven

The "Fifty-Fifty Club"

‑‑

From its inception, I tried everything possible to make the "Fifty-Fifty Club" a success. And from the mail that poured in, the telephone calls we received, the huge participation in the contests we ran, and the wonderful guests that we in‑ troduced to the audience, it was apparent that we were succeeding.

One day I mentioned that the large stick microphone that I used daily, and whose cord I was forever tripping over, was very drab and ugly. The next day my producer, George Resing, had it bedecked with a beautiful bouquet. This be‑ came a kind of symbol of mine on the show. Every day the women in the audience begged to have the flowers for their own. Since this was rather expensive, we finally settled on artificial flowers. There was a bow of ribbon with streamers attached. Nearly every florist in Cincinnati and Dayton com‑ peted with one another in making up these bouquets, and soon we had a cupboard full of them. We had special ones for certain occasions, such as holidays, and at other times to tie in with the theme of the show. We tried to use a certain theme throughout each show. Elsa Sule, assistant producer, was responsible for all of these efforts, and we celebrated everything from Washington's Birthday to Groundhog Day. We did many singing commercials, which I wrote for various products, from B-C to Kellogg's Corn Flakes.

I never worried about ratings, for I didn't consider them accurate, and I still don't. As long as I received sufficient mail in our various write-in promotions and contests, and as long as the sponsors were happy and contented with the increases in sales of their various products, I felt that we were doing all right. I continued in this attitude until the day I left, and we achieved a rating better than many nighttime shows.

I tried to keep up on all topical matters in the news and sports and to read nearly every new book that was printed, and when possible, interview the author. I recall that authors were, for the most part, rather difficult to interview. Although they might have written an excellent book, when they appeared on television with a live audience before them, they were, as a rule, very nervous. I considered it my job, having read their books, to put them at their ease, and by disagreeing on some issues with them, thus stimulating the conversation. An exciting interview often was the result. I learned that I shouldn't monopolize the conversation, but that I should rouse them to speak up and help them forget that they were under studio lights and on camera. They were grateful, as they told me later that they were very comfortable and felt that they had gotten their ideas across to the audience as never before. I never accepted an author to be interviewed unless his or her book promised to be as interesting to my audience as it had been to me.

To encourage comfortable conversation, I chose for our studio set a rocking—yes, rocking—love seat, with a large overstuffed rocking chair on either side for the announcer and vocalist. They were all in Early American style, as I have in my own home, for the studio was to become my home away from home. At first the engineers grumbled about my back and forth movements on the screen, especially when I took off on a controversial subject, when I really rocked. Some guests pretended they were seasick, but in time we all ended up very comfortable, and the engineers were reconciled.

I never used a written script on my show. At the far side of the studio was a large blackboard, and each day the commercials were posted there (in larger letters as I grew older). I had but to glance at them to see what commercials I had for that day, and as I included them in the show, one by one, the board became denuded. It seems I had a natural sense of timing from the old radio days, and also, most important to any show, a feeling of pacing. When an audience seemed to grow a bit restive, I would immediately change the subject, call on the band or vocalist, or present the commercials in a new way, by calling on someone from the audience to assist me. This kept the women responsive at all times.

It also seems that I had a penchant for transforming set-up boys into comedians. I always felt that they were a part of the show and that they contributed some of the funniest bits on the show. They would put up the wrong displays or pretend they didn't have the product I needed in the studio when the time came for me to do the commercial. Whenever I would sing a number, and I hasten to add, I am no singer, there were always loud crashes of dishes, falling objects, or a howling noise off the set. The boys loved to play all kinds of tricks on me. It got to the point that I feared to open the refrigerator door, a commercial highly regarded by our sales department, for fear of what might be in it—anything from an old pair of sneakers to an upset milk bottle dripping its contents. One morning each week one of the set-up boys took me to the beauty salon, and when he called for me, he would invariably ask, "Couldn't they take you?" Another time, having to wait for me a few minutes, he parked in a no parking zone. I came out and thought my car was on fire. The hood was up, and smoke was pouring from everywhere. Finally, this pixie emerged from under the hood, puffing furiously on a big cigar. The policeman on the beat, who after driving past several times, reappeared at the same time I did, and congratulated him on "fixing" his engine trouble. However, he got his comeuppance, for he turned slightly green on the way back to the studio.

The day I bought my first mink coat I was naturally very proud of it, and talked about it on the air. The women wanted to see it. I sent one of the boys to bring it from my office. I might have known that in its place would be brought a motheaten, raggedy coat, which we had purchased some years before for three dollars and left in the prop room.

Each day we gave a cake to someone who was celebrating a birthday, and it became a daily gag for Brady Lewis, a prop boy, later one of our salesmen, to take it to the recipient. He would juggle it about and then collapse into the lap of one of the women, pretending to trip as he dropped the cake. The first time he did it I nearly fainted. Then I found out that he had substituted for the beautifully iced cake a mock-up of the real cake.

The set-up boys worked hard, and I loved every one of them for all their assistance and help in setting up the studio every day and doing a million and one other things beyond the call of duty. They did the warm-up of the audience for about five minutes before every show, and one of them, Bill Gustin, became so proficient at his job, that I chose him to succeed George Resing, who had been my producer for ten years and was being moved up in the organization.

Speaking of producers, in those early days of television I

had a number of them before George. One, I remember vividly, came from New York with great recommendations, but he lasted only two weeks. I arrived at the studio one Memorial Day when we were to have a large group of servicemen on the show. We had decided the day before to put risers in the front of the studio in addition to the five tiers of seats for the audience. Although I seldom went into the studio before going to my office, on this particular day I did. I asked the set-up boys where the producer was, while they were rushing about like mad hanging the flag, getting the props together, and the band was rehearsing the servicemen. No one seemed to know. Upon entering my office, I found him, with his feet propped up on my desk, calmly reading the ads, "Apartments for Rent." In no uncertain terms I told him he wouldn't need an apartment in Cincinnati. That was the last broadcast he did for WLW-T. I realized then that only a local boy, who knew the show, the area, and most of all, me, would ever be successful as my producer. So I chose George Resing, who had just returned from Korea and was the head set-up boy. I never regretted this. George was not a "yes man," but he could always be relied upon for every detail and to put on a good show. Later, as I said before, Bill Gustin, who had worked closely with George, was chosen to succeed him.

One day our guest was a Negro singer, Arthur Lee Simpkins, who was appearing at the Beverly Hills night club. Herman and I had gone the night before to hear him, and he had a marvelous tenor voice for both serious songs and rhythm numbers. However, when he appeared on the show, he was extremely nervous when he sang his first number. I sensed this immediately, and in order to put him more at ease, I got up and went over to him, took him by the hand, and suggested that he sing his rhythm arrangement of

Arthur Lee Simpkins visits the show.

"Marie." The band started up with a good beat, and I danced for a few minutes with him. Well, I could never have anticipated the uproar this created. It was in 1952, long before the present day of Negro racial strife. One women wrote and said that I had degraded American womanhood by my action. I am happy to say, that not all reacted in this way—and I herewith quote from a telegram from one of those listeners:

Dear Ruth,
Your open heart made me cry tears of gratitude Tuesday when you so unreservedly demonstrated your heartfelt love for another human being, without being hampered one bit by the color of his skin. Such a spontaneous demonstration is sure to contribute more to racial harmony and good will than you have any idea.
God Bless you.
A viewer (white)

The next day I really took off on racial prejudice. I talked for a good fifteen minutes. The mail poured in after that "speech," and I found many people in our area in agreement with my views.

It is almost impossible to describe the events of the next few years. They started out quite routine enough, full of real enjoyment and many delightful experiences. The night club, Beverly Hills, across the river, brought into the Cincinnati area all of the big stars in show business, from whence came may of our guests, such as Sammy Davis, Jr. with his father and uncle. Sammy Davis, Jr. is a tremendous performer, and very likable. He stayed on the show for the full hour and a half, danced, sang, and did his gun tricks, for which he is famous. And I loved him. The Cincinnati Symphony Orchestra, as well as the Cincinnati Summer Opera,

Sammy Davis, Jr.

provided us with some truly fine talent. I have always been a sports fan and have been interested in the Cincinnati Reds, the U.C. basketball teams, Ohio State basketball, and various other sports and their leaders.

WLW-T was now a network of its own, having added a station in Dayton, Ohio, one in Columbus, Ohio, and finally WLW-I in Indianapolis, Indiana. Television was the big thing, and we were right in the middle of it. It was a time of trial and error. Meanwhile, radio seemed almost forgotten. Its heyday was usurped by people who were watching and not just listening. WLW was not content to have this happen, nor was I. With all of our television coverage, there was still a vast listening area in Ohio, Kentucky, Indiana, and West Virginia. So it was decided that the "Fifty-Fifty Club" should become a simulcast heard on radio at the same time that it was shown on television. Believe me, working this out wasn't easy. Everything that took place in front of the camera had to be done in such a manner that we could tell or explain it for radio as well. At first, from time to time, we had to remind ourselves that we were back on radio again, and it was very important to remember this. We even put up a sign on the studio door that read REMEMBER RADIO.

Returning to radio was like returning home for me. Our sponsors had to be sold on the idea, especially since the cost of each commercial increased. They kept faith with me, however, and we remained with the full schedule of commercials on the show.

About this time, through Mr. Murphy, it was arranged for me to be a guest for a week on the NBC "Today" show, presided over by Dave Garroway. This turned out to be a great disappointment to my audience. We had talked about it for weeks in advance, and everyone waited breathlessly for my appearance. But during the week I don't think they saw me more than two or three times. Most of the commercials on the show were either taped or seen only in certain sections of the country. I recall one commercial I was asked to do for a florist sale where I was completely banked by large potted plants, through which I peeked at the audience. My viewers had expected that I would chat with Dave Garroway in the same way in which they were accustomed to seeing and hearing me on my own show. Obviously they were disappointed, and I was shocked to find on my return to Cincinnati the furor that my visit had set up. For days, and even weeks, the newspapers and hundreds of letters from viewers, some sent to NBC, protested that I had been treated very shabbily by the entire network. Many such expressions came from around the country from friends I had made during the short period of time that I had been on the network with the "Fifty-Fifty Club." In vain I tried to explain to my audience that Dave and the entire cast, as well as representatives of NBC, were wonderful to me, but it was all to no avail!

A lovely thing happened on that trip, for which I shall be eternally grateful. Before leaving home, I had written to Eleanor Roosevelt and asked if I might meet with her on my visit to New York. I was overjoyed to receive a cordial note inviting me to lunch with her at her apartment. I arrived bearing a small vase full of violets. When I somewhat nervously presented it to her, I tipped the vase, and water spilled all over the floor. She was graciousness personified, and soon put me at my ease. The luncheon was interrupted frequently by her secretary, who was arranging a flight to Harrisburg, Pennsylvania, where Mrs. Roosevelt was scheduled to speak that evening. There was much discussion of what she should wear and what she should take with her. This was finally decided by the great lady herself, who said that she would wear what she had on and take nothing else. I was stunned,

I appear on the "Today" Show with Jack Lescoulie and Dave Garroway.

for she was wearing a knitted dress with a hemline obviously shrunk into scallops by the cleaners. I found most unusual the fact that Mrs. Roosevelt served each of us personally from a small side table, getting up and down from the luncheon table after each course. It was a novel and most wonderful experience. Mrs. Roosevelt was a warm, charming, and very knowledgeable woman, and I feel that I was indeed fortunate to have had the opportunity of meeting her.

Wonderful people from show business began to ask to be on our show. There was only one stipulation upon which we insisted. Each guest must entertain on the show, and no one was paid more than one dollar for each appearance. Among the first to make appearances were Gus Van, Ted Lewis, Tony Pastor, Xavier Cugat and Abbe Lane, and Guy Lombardo, who directed our studio band in the traditional "Auld Lang Syne." We also began having movie stars who were promoting pictures in which they were appearing, such as Roger Smith, Scott Forbes, Angie Dickinson, and many others. I had some of the most interesting guests in the country. And these guests came in goodly number without promise of food, drink, or reimbursement. They came in exchange for a mention of a latest record, a recently published book, an appearance in a local night club—all because the word had been spread around that "Fifty-Fifty Club" mentions paid off in big dividends. I never met with my guests before the program. They stayed in my office, watching the show, in order to get the feel of the show, and then came into the studio to visit and perform. I tried to make them seem very real people and friends to the listeners and viewers. They never spoke prepared pieces, performed and left, but stayed and participated, even in commercials. Those who heard or saw it will never forget Shelley Berman giving instructions for "removing" the cap from a bottle of a certain

Shelley Berman gives instructions for removing a bottle cap.

Mort Sahl appears on the show.

bath oil. Mort Sahl, after a stint on "Fifty-Fifty Club," told me that he wished his network appearances could be like this!

Roberta Sherwood, a frequent visitor to the show, has a warm spot in her heart for the "Fifty-Fifty Club" listeners and viewers. When her husband died, she received literally thousands of sympathy cards and notes from people who had met her and come to know her through her appearances on the program. This was one of her greatest consolations, and she asked to make a return visit to the "Fifty-Fifty Club" to offer a humble "thank you" to her friends in the Midwest.

Roger Smith, star of 77 Sunset Strip and another good friend of the "Fifty-Fifty Club," met with a serious accident at his home in California. As was my custom, I kept my audience thoroughly informed of his condition and progress. And during his illness, Roger Smith received so many cards and letters from the Midwest that he had the highest mail count at Warner Brothers Studios.

In June 1953 Candy, Herman, and I went to London to attend the Coronation of Queen Elizabeth II. Through pure happenstance, Mr. Murphy was in New York when a ticket drawing was made for six seats for Westminster Abbey. He, with the true luck of the Irish, drew one of the treasured tickets, which he gave to me. Bless him! My husband, who by this time was teaching at the University of Cincinnati, and my darling daughter, who was then just nine years old, were as excited as I was. Such preparations I had to make. One was obligated to wear to the Abbey for the Coronation service an evening dress, any color but black, and our heads had to be covered. I chose a gray faille dress, the first and only Christian Dior Original I ever owned.

On the day of the Coronation I had to be at the Abbey before 6 A.M. It was a cold, rainy morning, and Westminster

Roger Smith visits the "Fifty-Fifty Club."

Abbey is anything but a cozy place to be on such a day. Everything was perfectly arranged, down to the merest detail. The interior of the Abbey was an awesome sight, as flags of all nations and banners hung everywhere. My seat was immediately to the left of the throne, and I had a most advantageous view of the entire proceedings. Straight across from where I sat, the Queen Mother with her two grand-children and many attendants were seated. I shall never forget the thrill of the trumpets sounding, the long procession of peers and peeresses in their scarlet ermine-trimmed robes, and the sound of the magnificent Abbey organ. Here was world history in the making! The new Queen was more beautiful than I had ever dreamed her to be, and Prince Philip looked like all the princes that I had ever read about in fairy tales. The Coronation services were very long, but there was so much to see and hear. I was the envy of everyone sitting close to me because I had provided myself with two chocolate bars tucked into the top of my dress. Since I had had breakfast at 4:30 A.M.—they were, at high noon—a royal feast.

As we left the Abbey, the sun was shining, and I could see the thousands of people lining the thoroughfares, many of whom had spent the rainy night before sleeping there, some with nothing more than newspapers to cover them. The English are a sturdy breed, indeed. My driver did some miraculous maneuvering, and I reached the Dorchester Hotel, where my daughter and husband were in the viewing stands awaiting me. So I also got to see the royal coach in all its splendor, the Commonwealth dignitaries, and the royal platoons as if I were one of Her Majesty's subjects!

The United States had sent as representatives Chief Justice Earl Warren, General George C. Marshall, and Mrs. Fleur Cowles. Despite exalted positions, the British press criticized the selection of representatives of our government, offended that President Eisenhower did not see fit to attend. I can testify to this, for on Monday following the ceremonies, I was invited to attend a press conference being held with General Marshall. While we awaited his arrival, I noticed there were only British writers present. And when he came into the room, they made him feel very ill at ease. He said that he would answer any questions the reporters might like to ask. There was a deadly silence. I was seated in the front row, and I waited for the press to speak up. Still nothing happened. I felt this to be a deliberate affront to a great American and to a man whom I greatly admired. So, my temper rose, and in desperation, remembering having heard that Mrs. Marshall had been having some trouble with her back, I burst out, "General Marshall, how is your wife's back?" He answered me very kindly that she was feeling better, and thanked me for asking. From then on the other reporters took over, while I sat and fumed inwardly.

Later, we met General Marshall and Justice Warren in a very unusual way. We were all staying at the same hotel, the Grosvenor House. One evening we had been visiting Candy's godmother in her room, and she had ordered a celebrative bottle of sherry. We waited long for it to arrive and finally left for our rooms without benefit of its bouquet. As we neared the elevator, a formally attired waiter, carrying the bottle of Harvey's Cream and four sparkling glasses on a silver tray, loomed into view! With some embarrassment Herman signed for it, and we continued toward our rooms. When we neared them, there stood General Marshall, Justice Warren, and Mrs. Cowles. It seems that Mrs. Cowles had lost the key to her room. While I went to our room to call the porter for her, Herman poured sherry for the threesome, and they drank a patriotic toast to the good ol' U.S.A.

We still have in our home the two glasses from which General Marshall and Justice Warren drank—a Coronation treasure, indeed!

We stayed in London for three weeks. While there, we attended the Coronation Ball at the Savoy Hotel, which Winston Churchill attended. I had tea with Malcolm Muggeridge, the former editor of *Punch* magazine. I sent articles home to the *Enquirer* and to the *Cincinnati Post*. Venita Kelly, the fashion editor of the *Cincinnati Post,* was in London also. She took me to a fashion show. I also visited the BBC, where I finally met the woman, Mrs. Rose Buckner, with whom I had exchanged broadcasts during the war. I met Edwin Newman of NBC and Walter Cronkite of CBS, and Herman took Candy and me to Oxford to meet the Spicers, his former teacher and dear friends. This being my first trip to England, we enjoyed every moment of it and saw all the sights in true tourist fashion.

And then we went to Holland, Belgium, Luxembourg, and finally to Germany, where I looked up many American soldiers from our area stationed in Heidelberg and Cologne. We rode in a boat down the Rhine River, which reminded me a great deal of the Ohio River back home. Then we crossed into Switzerland, which remains my favorite European country, and drove from Lucerne to Geneva over the Alps and then on to Paris.

Paris was to me the fulfillment of a lifetime dream. I shall ever remember the majesty of Notre Dame Cathedral, the pristine white of Sacré Coeur, the Palace at Versailles, the one at Fontainebleau, the boat ride on the River Seine on the *Bateaux Mouche,* when Candy was given a navigator's license by the captain of the boat after "piloting" the boat for a stretch!

I had so much to tell my viewers that I could hardly wait

to get home. I shared every wonderful experience that I had had with them. It made me feel that nothing is impossible. Here was I, one of them, who had seen a queen crowned, had visited many marvelous places that they longed to see, and had talked with their sons, husbands, and brothers far away from home. And they loved it!

chapter eight

We Go into Color Television

In October 1957 the "Fifty-Fifty Club" was first shown in color. What an exciting time that was! The color dealers throughout the area were anxious to get things started. On the first day our show was in color, WLW had about twenty color televisions set up in a large hotel parlor, and all the officials of the city, the agency men, as well as the television critics were invited to view the show in color. We had a new set for the studio—once again Early American in design. The studio was repainted in many different shades of blue, and there was a pink piano, no less. We all chose our clothes with great care so that they would be harmonious with our surroundings. We just couldn't realize that all this was happening to us.

The sale of color sets in Cincinnati and Dayton soared to unanticipated heights. Since we had many men viewers also, the pubs were quite soon a favorite viewing place. And in the department and appliance stores, women gathered by the hundreds daily at the noon hour to see color television. Ours was the first locally originated show in color in the state of Ohio. Soon the "Paul Dixon Show," which was seen from 9 to 10:30 A.M., and the "Midwestern Hayride" on Saturday nights, went to color. And finally the NBC network started bringing us shows in color. WLW-TV was a pioneer once again. The audience on our show was intrigued, so I conceived the idea of having the audience wave "to the folks who were watching," and taping that part of the show, then playing it back so the women could see themselves on our color monitors in the studio after the show was over. This was a great thrill for them, since the ownership of color sets was not then preponderant throughout the area. However, it increased by leaps and bounds. Cincinnati became known as "Color Town U.S.A."

The women who attended the "Fifty-Fifty Club" were lovely to see. I had once mentioned that no woman was smartly dressed unless she was wearing gloves. This started a trend that has continued until today. Every woman who appeared on the show put on her white gloves, and when they waved on camera, they were the best dressed audience I have ever seen on television. I recall that even the little girls, from as young as two months old, came wearing their gloves. Even the engineers appeared one day proudly displaying white dress gloves.

We had to convince many sponsors that their products would look much more real than ever before. At first they began bringing in displays of their various packagings in black and white. Especially was this true of the out-of-town national advertisers. But we convinced them that to use the product "as is" was entirely satisfactory. Many of them came to Cincinnati, and were finally convinced that this was true. The engineers nearly exploded when I appeared one day in an all-white dress. We never insisted on the boys wearing light blue shirts instead of white (an early color TV myth!). With the increased lighting, properly placed, our engineering staff worked out beautiful true-to-life pictures. I never

New York, spring 1957. I discuss color television with Perry Como and two members of his cast, formerly of WLW, Jack Brown and Anne Ryan. Candy is at Mr. Brown's right.

Our first color TV show. Mary Wood of the Cincinnati *Post & Times Star* and Mayor Carl Rich watch us on monitors at the Gibson Hotel.

even changed the color of my make-up, except to use a slightly darker powder. I felt that our studio audience should see us exactly as we were and that the products should be presented "*à la naturel.*"

One day we heard that another show was starting on another network opposite ours. I urged my audience to watch it and to write me their reactions. On the first day that it was on, I left the studio and went into my office to see the show for myself. When I returned I said I did not believe we had anything to worry about—and this proved to be so, as the show lasted only a few months.

Now, the problem of getting guests for the show was completely reversed. It seemed that everyone who came to town in a stage show, appearing at a night club, who had a record to promote, or who was in a movie or a television show, or had written a book, wanted to appear on the "Fifty-Fifty Club." By that time the studio audience had increased to one hundred and thirty women a day, and the show was seen in Indianapolis, a station which Avco had recently acquired, as well as Columbus, Dayton, Cincinnati, and was also on radio. And what wonderful days those were, not only for my audience, but for me as well. The guests were fabulous, and they always complied with the rule that they must perform. I would never permit a singer to pantomime a record. Our band was a great one, and Cliff Lash, the leader, was a tremendous accompanist. I felt that the audience must hear as well as see the performer. Many of the performers I met stayed on to visit with me in my large, home-like office afterward. That office was beautiful—all done in shades of blue, Early American furnishings, a color television set, a record player, and boasting a large fireplace. And with the aroma of fresh-perked coffee, it indeed was their home away from home. I am sorry that my audience couldn't see it.

John Gary, a frequent guest and my favorite singer.

I really looked forward every day to doing the show. One of our earliest guests was John Gary, with whose lovely tenor voice I fell in love. He was on the show later many times. Then there was Peter Nero, the finest of all modern-day pianists. We plugged his album, and the sales were fantastic. Peter was then a newcomer to the Midwest, but very soon he became internationally known. Whenever he was near

My friend Peter Nero and I play *Tea For Two*.

Cincinnati he would come to play for us again and again. I consider him one of my dearest and most sincere friends. Another guest was the magnificent trumpeter, Al Hirt, who introduced his very first album on our show. And Johnny Mathis, who later recorded a song I wrote, "Wasn't the Summer Short?" with great success, as did Peter Nero. There were also the Four Saints, four very talented boys whose true potential has not yet been properly unveiled nationwide.

"Big Daddy" Al Hirt, who introduced his first album on our show.

Johnny Mathis, a very good friend indeed.

The Four Saints, frequent visitors to the "Fifty-Fifty Club."

When Van Cliburn appeared, and played the piano so magnificently, I found out that he had never learned to play "Chopsticks," so I sat down beside him on the piano bench, and we played it together. And with Jimmy Durante I played "Inka-Dinka-Doo." Victor Borge was a delight to my soul. We played the piano together, and finally he ended up underneath the piano, while I occupied the bench alone. I always watch for his rare appearances on present-day television. From Hollywood came Jack Webb and Troy Donahue, who was promoting his first starring role and who from that moment on became Candy's "big brother"—since he insisted Candy looked exactly like his younger sister. Others were Mort Sahl, Buddy Hackett, Jerry Lewis, Henny Youngman, Rosemary Clooney, the McGuire Sisters, and that beautiful man, Cesar Romero, with whom I danced, and could have danced all night. We also introduced Wayne Newton, who was just starting out; Efrem Zimbalist, Jr.; Cozy Cole and his group; and my great friend, Jack E. Leonard, who *can* be outtalked, as I proved. And I shall always remember Erroll Garner, who still never fails to remember me at Christmastime. From New York came Carol Channing, a very good friend of mine; Ezio Stuarti, with his marvelous voice; Lisa Kirk, Dorothy Sarnoff, the Four Aces, the Brothers Four, among many others.

Carol Channing came back several times, and when she was starring on Broadway in *Hello, Dolly!* she danced out onto the runway the night I was there and sang, "Hello, Ruthie!" to me. And there were the *Bonanza* boys, Hoss and Little Joe and Papa Cartwright. The day they came to town we were very thrilled. I wrote words to the tune of the *Bonanza* theme song to introduce them, and it delighted Lorne Greene. It was on our show that Little Joe first used a now oft-repeated phrase. When I asked him why he and

Van Cliburn.

the others never had a girl to take out, he said, "Try to get
the keys for the horse from Dad on a Saturday night." We
met the lovely Celeste Holm; my great favorites, the Buffalo
Bills; those crazy comedians, Steve Rossi and Marty Allen;
Lena Horne, who was as delightful as she is beautiful; and
two of my great favorites, Tom and Dickie Smothers.

Victor Borge.

Jimmy Durante plays Inka-Dinka-Doo.

Tab Hunter visits the Fifty-Fifty Club.

Henny Youngman instructs me on the violin, while Marian Spelman sings.

Erroll Garner, one of the nicest people I know.

I sing along with the Four Aces.

Buddy Hackett, whose father was an upholsterer, is complaining about the upholstery on my rocking chair.

My friend Carol Channing.

Miss Ethel Waters.

The great Bob Hope.

And there was the day that Robert Horton and I argued about his decision to leave the show that had brought him national recognition—the television show, *Wagon Train*—because he felt he was typed. I told him that I knew him not as Robert Horton, but as Flint McCullough, the part that he played in the television series. I had a marvelous interview with Miss Ethel Waters, who sang "His Eye Is on the Sparrow" for us, holding tightly to my hand all the while. She had been quite ill, and had made a great effort to appear. After her song there wasn't a dry eye in the studio. I first met Eydie Gorme and then later Steve Lawrence, both very talented young people. After the show Steve and I had a long talk in which he expressed his doubts as to whether, if he and Eydie married, their careers could continue successfully. I urged Steve to call Eydie in New York right then and there, and to date it has been a beautiful merger, both maritally and vocally. Bob Hope, that great and delightful man, appeared on the show and since then has successfully founded Hope House in Cincinnati, a home to help delinquent boys. And Julius La Rosa, I found, *did* have humility besides his great talent. I particularly enjoyed the visits with Pearl Bailey, Roger Williams, Florence Henderson, Bob Newhart, Woody Woodbury, Carmel Quinn, Frank D'Rone, the Harmonicats, and especially John Forsythe. I will never be able to decide who is the more handsome man, John Forsythe or Hugh O'Brian, with whom I struck up a wonderful acquaintance (Candy shared my indecision). When Steve Allen was on the show, he enjoyed a jam session so much with our band and with me at the organ, that although his managers were waving to him from the back of the studio to leave, since he had another engagement, he ignored them completely. And then came that utterly charming and courageous man, Arthur Godfrey. He returned several times to be on the show, de-

Michael Landon and Lorne Greene from *Bonanza* talk with Candy and me.

Celeste Holm, with Colleen Sharp at my right, and Peter Grant.

spite much opposition by a competing station which carried his radio show. I had met him previously in New York many years before, and had acquired from him a saying which I had made into a motto which hung on the walls of my office until I retired. This read: "Let me judge no man until I have walked in his moccasins for two months."

And I shall ever remember the time when Michael Ansara, the make-believe Indian on the television series *Broken Arrow*, was our guest. He was late in arriving, since he had made an appearance earlier at Coney Island that morning. I was talking about him on the show before he arrived, and I made the remark that I wondered if he shaved his chest, since Indians are supposed to have no hair there. The first thing he said to me upon entering the studio in full Indian regalia was, "No, I do not have hair on my chest." And he proceeded to open his shirt wide to prove it. For once I was speechless. He had been listening to the show on a car radio on his way to the studio.

There are two writers I have never forgotten. One of them is Hedda Hopper. It was around Christmastime, and trying to outdo Hedda's usual millinery magnificence, I had a large straw sailor hat gilded and topped with a miniature Christmas tree. After giving us all the latest gossip from Hollywood and telling us about the old-time movie stars she had known, she graciously accepted my hat. Later she wrote and told me she had worn it to a Christmas party in New York, and she sent me a fabulous hat in return. The other writer was Adela Rogers St. Johns. She came to town to promote the sale of her first book, *Final Verdict*. I loved that book, as well as its author. Mrs. St. Johns was a bundle of dynamite. After the show she appeared at Shillito's book department, where she sold and autographed over a thousand books that afternoon. And there were still several thousand orders tele-

The Buffalo Bills.

Tom and Dick Smothers.

phoned in, besides the ones to come in Dayton, Columbus, and Indianapolis.

When Sam Levinson was on the show, the conversation was most stimulating, and later, when he returned, he was so kind and sympathetic that we both broke down and cried. I am very happy that he has been so successful, for with all his subsequent success in writing, he is a most modest gentleman much to be admired.

Liberace once rode with me in a Rolls-Royce from the hotel to the auditorium where we had taken our show to do a remote. Andy Williams appeared on stage with the show in Columbus, Ohio, as did Johnny Desmond.

Every year we did a remote in one of the other cities which carried the show, and for those days we offered two tickets per person. The women who already had purchased tickets for these days received others for a later date before the next regular ticket sale. We always appeared in the largest available hall in each city, and although we could only seat 4200 persons, as a general rule our ticket requests ran to more than 40,000. Remotes were always great fun, with a motorcade, flanked by motorcycle police, from the hotels to the auditoriums. The stages were beautifully decorated with baskets of flowers, and most delightful of all, this gave us the opportunity to go down the aisle and shake the hands of hundreds of women, many of whom had waited since dawn to meet us. We always had the governors of the states on the show; in Ohio, Governor C. William O'Neill, Governor Michael V. DiSalle, and Governor James Rhodes. And when we went to Indianapolis, Governor Roger Branigan visited us. The mayors of the cities also appeared on the show and presented me with the keys to the city and the usual scrolls of honor. It seems that they tried to outdo one another in the number of *whereas*'s contained in each scroll. I would often comment

Roger Williams visits the show and sits on phone books reserved for
Erroll Garner. Peter Grant is at my right.

Arthur Godfrey. "Let me judge no man until I have walked in his moccasins for two months."

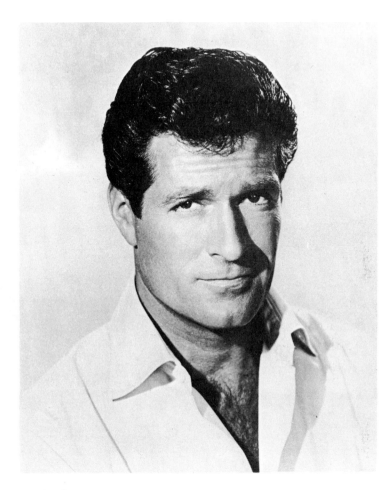

Hugh O'Brian.

I present Hedda Hopper with a Christmas hat, which she wore down Fifth Avenue in New York on Christmas Day.

Liberace signing the guest book in my office.

Adela Rogers St. Johns discusses *Final Verdict*.

Henry Cabot Lodge appears on the "Fifty-Fifty Club" during the 1960 campaign.

on this, and it always brought a great laugh from the audience. I appreciated the hospitality, however, as well as the wonderful treatment by the hotel managements where we spent the night before. The telephone would start to ring the minute we arrived, gifts were delivered to us from viewers who had not gotten tickets to the show, and we were made to feel very much at home, away from home.

In 1960, the year of the presidential election, John F. Kennedy and Lyndon B. Johnson were running on the Democratic ticket. And on the Republican ticket were Richard M. Nixon and Henry Cabot Lodge. I had invited Henry Cabot Lodge and his opponent, Lyndon Johnson, to make an appearance on the "Fifty-Fifty Club." Mr. Lodge came, but Mr. Johnson sent a telegram which we read in its entirety, stating that he would be unable to appear because of previous commitments. The day before Lodge arrived, the building swarmed with Secret Service men and producers who insisted that the cameras "shoot" him from certain angles and that he could not sit on the rocking love seat. This went on all day. Finally I blew up and told them that the "Fifty-Fifty Club" was my show and that it would be conducted just the same as any other day. When Mr. Lodge arrived for the telecast, he was charm itself and most cooperative. We rocked back and forth together, and he made a terrific interview, and from his party's position—a great vote-getting one!

My audience was always conjecturing about my political affiliations. A newspaperwoman wrote an article, which I quote herein, as well as my answer to her. The cartoon appeared in her paper on the same day.

An Open Letter to Ruth Lyons *asks her to state convictions*

Dear Ruth:

On last Monday's show, October 24, you stated that you had been invited by both political parties to share the platform with their standard bearers when they appeared in Cincinnati. Doesn't this seem a bit odd? Not since Harry Truman tried to corral Dwight Eisenhower have both parties been after the same man, or woman, as in your case!

You stated that you could not accept either offer, even though it was a signal honor, since you wanted to have a job on November 9. You said you could not express yourself since you would be interfering with the political life of your friends. Could it be that you are simply refusing to stand up and be counted?

My dear, do you believe that your friends are so fickle as to tune you out, or what you fear most, quit buying your products, if your stated political belief is different than theirs? I have been an admirer and friend of yours for years because you have always had the courage of your convictions, even though they sometimes didn't agree with mine. Now, my respect has fallen because I believe you are not nearly so concerned about the state of our country as you are about the state of Ruth. Do you speak out only when it doesn't concern you or yours? Are your convictions strong only when they don't touch you personally?

As a Republican, my esteem of you will be higher, if you declare yourself a member of the Democratic party (if you are), or Republican party (if you choose) than if you hurt the two-party system under which we operate by not stating a firm belief in either. You know as well as I do that the so-called independent voter is the most dependent of all, since he must live under a policy chosen by someone else. Whether you are Republican or Democrat, you should be willing to state your position. That is not to say, that you will use your airtime to argue either side. Your friends know of the station policy of equal time. This is not the point in issue. It is simply, where do you stand!

Surely, Ruth, in this enlightened world in which we live, there is room for complete honesty. To believe, and not to say you believe, is a sin of omission just as sinful as a sin of commission. You have been so outspoken on other matters, which had not the importance of this one, I know you did not intend to show indecisive self-centeredness here.

Sincerely,
Dorothy Franke

A Wide Open Letter to Dorothy Franke

No, Dorothy, I am not refusing to "stand up and be counted" as to my political affiliations or interests in this most important national election. I simply remind you of the sanctity of the American voter, the right and the validity of the secret ballot.

I am an employee of the Crosley Broadcasting Corporation. As such, I am not in a position, nor do I wish to be, of trying to influence any American citizen as to how he or she should cast a ballot on November 8. No television or radio station, to my knowledge, backs any political candidate or party. It is our duty to inform the public on all issues as fairly as possible and without bias, regardless of any employee's personal convictions. I believe that American newspapers and periodicals should follow a like procedure. I have never approved of the practice wherein a newspaper "comes out" for a particular party or candidate. I believe all information about their activities should be reported, not advocated or denounced according to the personal feelings of an editor or personally dictated editorial policy.

On my program I have an enviable opportunity to do one

thing: to try desperately to attempt to get our great Midwest population interested in issues and problems that every American must examine and face today. I have the right, as a human being, to urge everyone to use his or her opportunity to vote; to consider seriously the devastating effects of bigotry against race, creed or color; to call attention to the people to the need for support of the aged, the mentally incapacitated, the some time forgotten sick children, the dangers of hypocrisy, false advertising, and a number of other vitally important matters that are often overlooked or ignored in today's hectic pattern of living.

I do not assume that my fine, intelligent audience joins me daily, or, as you suggest, would ignore me daily if I were to declare my personal political convictions. When our Christmas Fund is distributed, when the toys purchased from it are placed in the hands of a little sick child, we do not ask, "Did your father or mother vote Democratic or Republican?" "Are you a Catholic or a Protestant or a Jew?" "Are you of the Caucasian or the Negro race?"

When the women of my audience are told of many commercial products, which they may or may not be inclined to try, do they first ask themselves, "Is this a product manufactured by a company that is primarily Democratic or Republican?" I think not, nor do I think that I would be any less effective or more kindly received by these good people, if I made it a point to announce or expound upon my political feelings.

You question my honesty. Can I be any more honest than I have tried to be during my 32 years in the radio and television industry? If so, then your concept of honesty and mine differ considerably. My definition of honesty includes the importance of preserving the dignity of the individual, in regard to political interpretation, religious belief, the right to a personal approach to solve one's own problems, assist those less fortunate than one's self, in short, to live as much as possible by the "Golden Rule," not spasmodically, but daily.

I wish to present to our television and radio audiences guests from the entertainment field, doctors, people who write, and other fields of interest, and even those who are in the position of running for the highest office in the United States. Could I fairly, honestly, and without prejudice talk with these guests, particularly those in the political field if I had previously avowed or disavowed my position on what they believe or advocate?

You inferred, in your open letter to me, that I was concerned only for my own well-being, not for the state of the country and the world. It is because I believe in the judgment of the American voting public and the two-party system, the right of the individual to determine his decisions that I refrain, and sometimes with difficulty, from declaring my own position, lest I use our large television and radio facilities to influence the individuals in our audience in any way, especially in matters that are inherently personal ones.

No, Dorothy, I do not believe that I have the right, nor the desire, to try in any manner to influence the vote of any American citizen, simply because I happen to have made my own determination as to how my lone vote shall be cast. When I walk into that voting booth, I do not want anyone looking over my shoulder, giving me a nod of approval or a frown of disapproval. My vote is my own, as yours is yours. Let's keep it that way.

Sincerely,
Ruth Lyons

There were many times that I had to go on the air with a heavy heart. One in particular happened late in 1959. I had a young secretary, who because of a frustrated love affair, had become despondent. When she began missing work quite a bit, I finally asked Mr. Dunville to send her to a secretarial school, which he did. But it was inevitable that this was not working. I finally found her a job with another company and kept in touch with her constantly. However, we lost her eventually. It was a dreadful thing for all of us. We were in the midst of raising the Christmas Fund for that year, and we all loved her very much. She had worked in my office for nearly fourteen years.

I also had the additional sorrow of knowing that my sister had cancer. I brought her to work for me, and she had charge of the various ticket sales, as well as helping with the counting of the money for the Christmas Fund. She was full of life and had a wonderful sense of humor. But there were many trying days, watching my sister grow thinner each day and doing all I could to keep my own spirits up as well as hers. However, the show must go on, at least that is what they say. I do not subscribe entirely to this belief, but I suppose I had an innate sense of trying to do all that I could to keep the "Fifty-Fifty Club" going to the best of my ability.

The presidential election was won by John F. Kennedy and Vice-President Johnson, as you know. And we began once more the raising of the Ruth Lyons' Christmas Fund. We had many great guests who graced our show and with whom I especially enjoyed talking. One of our guests was Sargent Shriver, who had been made the head of the Peace Corps and was later appointed our ambassador to France. He is a charming man in every respect.

We also had the pleasure of interviewing Miss Helen Hayes. She was greatly and deservedly loved by all, not only for her great talent as an actress, but as a genuine person.

Ed Ames was another great guest, and his singing is unequaled. He feels the words of his song, as well as the music. When he sang "Time to Remember" from *The Fantasticks,* it was indeed a time to remember!

Miss Helen Hayes.

Ed Ames, another great friend.

When Eva Gabor appeared, the most feminine woman I have ever seen, she was wearing a huge thirteen-carat diamond ring. I asked her if it was real, and her reply was typically Eva. She said. "Vhy, yes, vhen I am vorking and making money, I vear it. Vhen I am not vorking, it iss—how you say it—in hock."

One day when Mayor Charles P. Taft, son of former President William Howard Taft, dropped in for a visit, the conversation turned to the somewhat complicated Taft family tree. "And there was my uncle who was born in Lytle Park," said Mayor Taft. "Well," I answered, "it does happen. Sometimes you just can't make it to the hospital on time." The Mayor managed to explain that he meant a house in our downtown section, now called the Taft Museum, and where formerly Lytle Park was located.

When one of the vocalists on the show, Marian Spelman, who has a lovely voice and is lovely to look at, made her musical comedy debut in *Wonderful Town*, I hired a bus and we all went to Dayton, Ohio, for her opening night. According to Marian, I got a bigger ovation than she did, which is not true. She was a great success!

I was always very pleased when any member of my cast, the singers, Marian Spelman, Ruby Wright, or Bonnie Lou, made a success in some other undertaking. Ruby had a hit record in the revival of "Thanks for the Buggy Ride." Bonnie Lou sang her first popular rhythm tune on the show, and thus enlarged her repertoire from the country and Western music which she usually sang. I remember what a great thrill that was for us all.

And I was indeed proud when my dear Candy was given a small part in *Palm Springs Week-end*, starring her idol Troy Donahue. I took her to California, where we were treated royally by Warner Brothers Studios. From that time on, Candy always called Frank Casey, who is in charge of the Chicago office for Warner Brothers, her "Santa Claus." He had made possible for her a priceless gift.

I once spent an evening at the Shrine Circus with Richard M. Nixon, who talked about very little except his wife and children and my work in the Cincinnati area.

How I enjoyed the day Milton Berle was on the show! He stayed after the show for several hours, and he was a true delight as we discussed music, his early career, and show business in general.

When Phyllis Diller made any of her many appearances, the entire audience completely broke up. Offstage she is a very intelligent and oft-times serious person.

Many other fine guests visited us as well. George Kirby came and candidly told us of his long personal battle against drug addiction. He sang and joked and laughed with us, and we all took him to our hearts. And there were also Jim Backus, Tony Bennett, Viveca Lindfors, Rod Serling, who was formerly a script writer at WLW. I shall never forget the incomparable Duke Ellington, who played "Sophisticated Lady" for us and was very charming, as was that great gentleman, Cab Calloway. Our audience also had the pleasure of meeting Sarah Vaughan, Dizzie Gillespie, A. J. Foyt, the winner of the Indianapolis 500 racing classic; Margaret O'Brien, Mel Tormé, and many, many others too numerous to mention.

We especially fell in love with the great South African golfer, Gary Player, as well as many baseball stars, basketball stars, their coaches and their managers.

In time the women in our audience became very sports-minded. In 1961, the Cincinnati Reds won the National League pennant. Every day, near the end of the exciting race for first place, we sang a parody I had written, "Let's Rally Round the Reds." And I took full credit for their winning

Dancing with Milton Berle.

Phyllis Diller always kept us laughing.

Cab Calloway.

Governor Nelson A. Rockefeller.

Douglas Fairbanks, Jr. visits the Fifty-Fifty Club. At left is Bonnie Lou, vocalist, and next to me is Ann Baxter.

the pennant, saying that I had a direct telephone line into the Reds' dugout and that I did most of the coaching with my dear friend, the late Fred Hutchinson, the regular manager. Also that year the University of Cincinnati basketball team won the NCAA championship, under the superb leadership of Coach Ed Jucker. They won it again the next year, and were beaten by only two points by Loyola University in the year following. We had all the players of the Reds team on the show, as well as the boys from the University basketball team. The remarkable Oscar Robertson, whom I consider to be the greatest basketball player ever, was a guest on the show several times. Ed Jucker now coaches the Cincinnati Royals team, which at last report was doing splendidly. When Ohio State, with their superb Jerry Lucas, John Havlicek, and Mel Nowell, were basketball champions, we shared their glory with our audience also. Our band had arrangements of all of the various school songs, and there was much rivalry during those years.

But all was not sports. About this time Otto Preminger made a guest appearance, as did David Merrick, Larry Blyden, Emily Kimbrough, who discussed her latest book; Hildegarde, Dorothy Collins, Paul Anka, and Doris Day, who originally lived in Cincinnati. Also appearing were Bob Clary, who now plays in *Hogan's Heroes* on television and who was a true delight, and the late Dorothy Dandridge.

I shall never forget when the Zoo Summer Opera stars began their season in Cincinnati. We all fell in love with Sherrill Milnes, laughed with Salvatore Baccaloni, especially when he advised us that the only medicine he ever took, upon the advice of his doctor in Italy, was brandy.

Vivienne della Chiesa, who now has an afternoon television show on WLW, was also our guest, as was Barry Morrell. I had a joke of long-standing with Barry. He had been on the

I coach the Cincinnati Reds to the pennant, from the dugout at Crosley
Field.

Vivienne della Chiesa.

show a few weeks before we went into color television. That summer I had broken my toe when I hit it on the diving board of our swimming pool. Since there was nothing that the doctor could do to help it heal except to let nature take its course, I was doing just that, until one day when Barry was on the show, he inadvertently stepped on my foot. I nearly fainted! Barry apologized profusely, but he never quite forgave himself. And he kept on apologizing each time he subsequently appeared on the show, even to the point of having a plaque made up making me a member of the "Broken-Toe Society." After my mishap with Barry, I made quite a thing of that broken toe. I had to wear a pair of white thongs, which I had decorated with flowers and tiny bells whose jangling nearly drove the engineers crazy, but these histrionics had the desired effect and elicited a great deal of merriment from the audience.

Who can ever forget the visit of Dick Powell and his lovely wife June Allyson. Dick had just come to the studio from a doctor, who said that he had a severe case of hives caused by medicine he was taking. His throat was very swollen, and he could scarcely talk. WLW-T had a luncheon for them after the show, and I could see that he was in great discomfort. They flew back to Hollywood that afternoon, and Dick died several weeks later from cancer of the throat. No one would have sensed on the day that he appeared that he was suffering so severely.

Dr. Nelson Glueck, the president of Hebrew Union College, came to introduce his book, *Rivers in the Desert,* and we discussed many of his marvelous adventures in the Holy Land. Dr. Glueck sold many books later at an autographing session at Shillito's. He visited the show several times afterward, humbly impressed with the marked interest of our audience in his scholarly works.

Dick Powell, making his last appearance, with his lovely wife June Allyson.

The author Victor Lasky was widely criticized for his book about President Kennedy, which he later withdrew from sales by his own choice. However, when he came as a guest to publicize his book, *The Ugly Russian,* I found Mr. Lasky a highly informed, delightful person, and we got along famously.

There was one author whose book I enjoyed thoroughly. It was all about early Cincinnati and the early whiskey industry, among other things. It was called, curiously enough, *The Water of Life.* The author was Henry Morton Robinson, and when talking with him, I said he must have done a great amount of research on Cincinnati. He said he had only spent twenty minutes here, between trains, about twenty years before. For once I was struck almost speechless. His book was certainly not among the best sellers. (By tragic coincidence, a few years later he fell in his bathtub of scalding water and drowned.)

About this time something happened that greatly disturbed the studio, my family especially, and a little later on, the audience. One day one of my secretaries, Sue, opened a letter from someone who threatened my life. The FBI, under the supervision of Mr. Ed Mason, was called in, and we found that the life of President Kennedy had also been threatened. The handwriting on the letter to me was identical to that on the one sent to the President, another to Police Chief Stanley Schrotel, and Colonel Henry Sandman, chief of detectives. The newspapers printed the letters on the front page, and people were asked to try to identify the writing. They asked me if I wanted to go away until the person was apprehended, but I continued the show as usual. WLW had an around-the-clock police guard at my home. Even the cab drivers, who drove me back and forth to the studio, had to be cleared by the FBI. This lasted for more than three weeks. Sixty-five

FBI agents worked on an all-night basis, with no weekends or holidays off. They checked the handwriting and printing through 470,000 files of the Veterans Administration, through hospital files, through probation records, and 114,000 selective service applications. Then they started checking library cards, and after examining 70,000 of them, they found what they had been looking for. The perpetrator was a young man, twenty-four years old, who after psychiatric examination, was declared to be mentally unstable, having been dismissed from the military service for this reason. The reason the FBI was called in and handled the case so expertly was because of the threat to President Kennedy by the same man. He was committed to a federal mental institution. I shall be eternally grateful to the FBI and to our local police department for their devoted efforts on behalf of me and my family.

I have since received several other strange letters from other persons, which when checked out, all proved to be from persons afflicted with mental illness. So you can understand why it is not all pleasure to be a celebrity in your own home area.

Late in 1963 Troy Donahue came to Cincinnati to appear at the opening of the picture, *Palm Springs Week-end,* the picture in which Candy had a small part. Troy and Frank Casey of Warner Brothers had dinner with us on Thursday night, after being on the show that day with Jayne Mansfield and Henny Youngman. On Friday when the "Fifty-Fifty Club" ended, I went to my office and picked up the telephone to make a call. The WLW operator told me to turn on the television set immediately. That was when I heard the first report of the assassination of President John F. Kennedy. Almost in a daze, I rushed home immediately, and for the next three days I never left the television set. The shock and disbelief were almost too much to bear.

Troy Donahue and Jayne Mansfield.

When I returned to the air on Tuesday it was a very difficult time. I was outraged and grieved, as so many Americans were. I had the American flag fill the entire television screen at the start of the program, and I just tried to say what I knew millions of Americans were trying to say, had they had the same opportunity that was afforded me. I cannot possibly remember my exact words, but they were straight from my heart. Here are some excerpts from letters that I received after that broadcast. One writer was a prominent minister who said in part:

Just a line of appreciation for the touching manner in which you commented on Tuesday, November 26. Only a woman—and that woman, Ruth Lyons—could have summarized so pointedly the meaning of the millions of words that we listened to during the past few heartbreaking days, especially when you said, "God wept at the tragedy of Dallas." What you were exposed to as a small child at the old Sixth Presbyterian Church must have made a lasting impression. Your reference to the deplorable fact that no minister was willing to give Oswald a Christian burial was well said. There was a young wife, her son, and a mother at the grave, whose destinies were still in the making. I rejoice that you gave the public a true understanding of what they have a right to expect of a minister of the gospel.

Another letter read:

Today was a most difficult day for you to open the program. How I admired you and agreed with your beautiful remarks, all given without a line of script. Most of all, I was impressed with your profound comments that I had heard no one give during the entire television coverage. This was the emphasis you placed on the Christian concept of condemning the *deed* Oswald had committed, but trying to forgive the *man*. This was obviously a working principle of the late John F. Kennedy. Thank you also for calling on the Church to live up to its responsibility to promote complete human equality. You are making an outstanding contribution every day to this cause. Always speak out loud and clear, Ruth. We are listening, and we are trying. I think you should re-run the show during the evening hours so that your many men listeners might hear it. We all needed to be reminded that peace in our nation, which walks proudly, was not dead, but had merely stumbled. We needed to be reassured of the faith we must have in our country and in ourselves. You assured us. We needed to be told (simply but firmly) that we must go on.

I had been written about in many national magazines. Writers came from New York and from Cincinnati and wrote their impressions of me and the show. The *American Home* magazine did quite an impressive picture feature on my home. One of my viewers who made a trip to Jamaica and visited the home of Noël Coward, saw the magazine on his coffee table.

I was honored by articles in *Look* magazine, *Saturday Evening Post,* and *Cosmopolitan* as well. Jack Douglas, in an article in *Radio-TV Daily,* wrote as follows:

The Ruth Lyons Show, "The Fifty-Fifty Club," runs ninety minutes daily. It can spot any comparable network show ten rating points and still win by ten. And for my money, Ruth Lyons is the most amazing woman now performing in television. No other woman in the country can even begin to match the fantastic-true legends that she has created. She is also the most delightful chatterbox I've ever seen on the tube. Paar and Godfrey combined wouldn't stand a chance at the same table.

165

Although this was quite flattering, I decided I would write my own story in my own words for the *Ladies' Home Journal.* I called the story "Life Has a Lovely Way of Living" —a line from one of my own Christmas songs. The results were amazing. It was almost impossible to buy a copy of the magazine anywhere in our area. Copies were shipped in to Cincinnati from Chicago, Cleveland, and other places, to help fulfill the demand. It was the largest magazine sale that the *Journal* ever had. It gave me great satisfaction, for it was my opportunity to write about what I believed, as well as give credit to my great audience, guests, and fellow workers. Once again I heard from many former viewers who had moved away from the area and had read the article. Nielsen and other rating services showed that we had a higher rating than many nighttime network shows and that I had also done more hours in color television than any other person in the country.

I have always had an excellent relationship with the area press—Mary Wood, of the *Post & Times-Star;* Dale Stevens, the former music critic of the same paper; Myrtie Barker, of the *Indianapolis News;* Mary Lee Wilman, of the *Kokomo Indiana Times;* and Gee Mitchell, of the *Dayton News.* At one time there was a feature writer for the old *Times-Star* who felt obliged to find fault with everything that I did on the show. I simply ignored his cruel remarks (and they were sometimes cruel), until he could stand it no longer and called our publicity department to find out why I never mentioned his name on the air or replied to his comments. They told him that I never read his column. He later became reconciled.

Our great guest list continued without abatement. There was Dr. Albert Sabin, who came to tell of his great oral vaccine against polio. Former Governor DiSalle came to discuss his views against capital punishment, about which he had

Herman and I in our garden.

I am with our housekeepers, Pauline Watson and Callie Borum.

written a book. Dick Contino appeared several times, and pleased our audience greatly with his rendition of "Battle Hymn of the Republic." And Oscar Peterson, that wonderful pianist, played for us several times.

We had a great gag going on the show. The song "I Love Paris" was one of my favorites. I would sing it whenever the occasion arose, and many times when it didn't. The trombone player in our band, Eddie Bennett, resorted in every way to drown me out. The band would give me a terrific introduction, then they would play quite softly during most of the song. But when I reached the climax, pandemonium broke loose. It was me against the band full force. Every pianist who appeared was put to the task of trying to help me. These included my friends (?) Peter Nero, Oscar Peterson, Skitch Henderson, Erroll Garner, and many others. Even Pete Fountain brought his clarinet and tried to help me. Also Tony Pastor tried to direct the band and to keep them under control. But it was all in vain. Even Al Hirt, with his overpowering trumpet, could not subdue Eddie. Doc Severinson also tried in vain, although he brought his entire group with him. It came to be a feature on the show, and no matter who our guest was for the day, the audience would demand that I sing "I Love Paris."

I enjoyed so many of our great guests in those days. Hugh Downs, of NBC's "Today" show, was delightful. And who will ever forget Eddie Albert, when he recited with a musical background, the lovely ballad, "Lasca," by Frank Desprez. Earl Wrightson and Lois Hunt were two of my favorite guests, and I pretended to sing with Earl. As usual, this turned out to be havoc.

Pat O'Brien came to talk about his sensitive book, *The Wind at My Back*. His lively Irish humor, in telling about his early struggles in Hollywood and New York and his later

Skitch Henderson, who tried to help me sing "I Love Paris."

Hugh Downs, of the NBC "Today" Show.

success, made a great hit with the viewing and listening audience, and he sold many books throughout our viewing area.

I happened to read a nostalgic book by Jean Shepherd, who is a late-night radio personality in New York, as he had been years before in Cincinnati at WLW. I was enchanted by the book. It is seldom one laughs aloud when reading a book, but I did just that in many parts of his book, which he called *In God We Trust—All Others Pay Cash*. The book concerned his boyhood in Indiana. I asked him to come to Cincinnati and be a guest on the "Fifty-Fifty Club." He enjoyed renewing many old acquaintances while he was here. The interview was a lot of fun, and I am sure that Jean sold many copies of his book, to his great delight.

And then came Lena Horne. Lena had written a book about her early rejection by the show world, her friendship with Medgar Evers and Dr. Martin Luther King. She was most passionate, and rightly so, about the plight of the Negro. What a beautiful woman she was! She was much more beautiful than when I had first met her several years before on the show. She was very nervous at first, but from the moment she faced the cameras, she relaxed completely. Lena wound up by singing "Stormy Weather" for us. Her book was a great success also, and she wrote me a charming letter of gratitude.

We had hired a hairdresser from Shillito's Beauty Salon, Dana Bruce, for Miss Horne. Mr. Bruce became very important to all of our girls in the office, our vocalists, and especially to me and my daughter. He gave the girls a course in make-up and provided many of us with wigs and wiglets, which were then becoming the rage.

One day he came on the show and made up Candy, complete with a blond wig, false eyelashes, and rather heavy eye-liner. I was not prepared for the reaction this had on our audience. Hundreds of letters, many of them from college students (male), poured in. Of course, it was an exaggerated make-up, but Candy did look lovely, and quite different. Many commented upon the striking resemblance to the late Marilyn Monroe.

In 1964 Horst Jankowski, who wrote "A Walk Through the Black Forest," visited the show, and how we did enjoy his piano playing. We also had Eartha Kitt that year, Allen and Rossi, Eddie Arnold, the late Frank Lovejoy, Johnny Tillotson, June Valli, Jean Paul Vignon, Juliet Prowse, Al Martino, and a return visit from Arthur Godfrey. That year also we met for the first time, John Davidson, who was just starting out on his career and has since become a nationally known favorite. Milton Caniff, the cartoonist, was also one of our guests. His mother lived in Ohio and was a daily viewer, according to Milt.

Our audiences were wonderful. We were sold out for nine years in advance at one time, but on the last ticket sale we sold tickets for only three years ahead. People ran ads in the newspapers offering to pay a premium price for tickets. One group came with tickets badly charred, which were the only things saved when the woman who had gotten them, carried them, and them alone, from her home, which fire had completely destroyed. Several of the viewers who had gotten tickets earlier had even bequeathed them in their wills.

I vividly remember the most embarrassing thing that ever happened to me on the show. Carmen Dragon, the fine conductor, was to be our guest. He was conducting a concert that weekend in Cincinnati. We talked for a bit, and then I asked him if he would play the piano for us. He insisted that he didn't play piano—but I thought he was just being modest. I was so insistent that he perform, that he finally went to the piano and played a few chords. It was obvious that he was not a pianist. Then—the light dawned! I had confused him

John Davidson visits the show and charms Candy and me.

Eddie Arnold.

all along with Carmen Cavallaro, whom I had met many, many years before in my early radio days. I couldn't insult Mr. Dragon by saying that I thought he was someone else, so I wound up our interview very quickly and spent the rest of the day feeling very foolish. I have often wondered what that dear man thought about the confused blonde in Cincinnati.

In June my only sister lost her ten-year battle with cancer. The last months were trying ones for all of us. I spent nearly every day at the hospital, and we talked for hours on the telephone. However, she died rather suddenly while I was just starting the show. They brought me a message to come to the hospital immediately. She was dead when I arrived, and at peace at long last.

Came October and we were well into raising the Christmas Fund again. It looked very hopeful. The Kroger Company, who was one of my sponsors, and who had built a new building in downtown Cincinnati, displayed the daily total in large neon letters on the top floor windows. And anyone driving into Cincinnati from any suburb or from across the river in Kentucky could keep up with the amount as it grew. This added a helpful dramatic flourish to our efforts.

We had many other great guests during this year. There were Edward Everett Horton, Wally Cox, Shani Wallis, Imogene Coca, Greg Morris and Michael Callan, and Lily Daché, who later sent me a white leather hat, which one of the girls in my office still has. We also entertained the Osmond Brothers, from the "Andy Williams Show"; Ilka Chase, who had written another book; the beautiful Barbara McNair, Frankie Laine, Tommy Leonetti, Count Basie, and Jack Carson. How we laughed at Molly Picon when she told us about her early childhood and the adventures she had had in the Yiddish theatre. Dick Clark also came to visit us,

176

as did Bobby Rydell, and that marvelous violinist, Florian Zabach, who returned many times later.

I shall never forget the way we laughed the day Michael Flanders and Donald Swann appeared. They were two Britishers making their first appearance in America. I completely broke up every time I looked at Donald Swann, and they seemed to enjoy the fun as well. Ferrante and Teischer brought their own two pianos and played for us. The Williams Family, from the ice show, were great favorites with our audience, and they came back every year to see us. Homer and Jethro, who had formerly been with me on the early morning radio show, just about dissolved me and the audience in laughter when they did some of the commercials.

We were greatly awed by Charlton Heston, who came to promote his great role in *The Ten Commandments,* as though it needed any promotion. I personally enjoyed our visit with Tony Randall, whose wit and charm completely captivated everyone. Anita Bryant returned several times, as she was a great friend of mine. Guy Marks taught us the song, "Your Red Scarf Matches Your Eyes," which has just been re-released and is now heard on the radio daily.

The women in the audience really enjoyed meeting Dale Robertson. Walter Slezak and I laughed through the whole show, as I did with Jack Carson. Jane Morgan, who has the most beautiful skin I have ever seen, was captivating. Later I met her in Las Vegas, where she introduced me to Mr. Jack Benny, with whom she was working at that time. Connie Haines came and sang for us, as did Sheila and Gordon MacRae. Phil Ford and Mimi Hines were truly delightful.

I thought I had found a wife for Peter Grant when Kaye Stevens appeared. She tried very hard to win Peter over, but, as usual, her blandishments were in vain. Among the funniest guests that we ever had were Joe Flynn and Tim Conway of

Florian Zabach.

Homer and Jethro, performing a commercial.

Tony Randall.

Joe Ross and Fred Gwynn introduced "Car 54" on the Fifty-Fifty Club.

Walter Slezak and I had a wonderful time.

McHale's Navy. Whenever I see them on the reruns today, I remember the wonderful time we had together. *Car 54* featured Joey Ross and Fred Gwynn. And they came to introduce the show on the "Fifty-Fifty Club."

We also had as guests Dick Kallman, Carol Lawrence, who as you know, is now married to that dreamboat, Robert Goulet; Dick Curtis, who worked at one of our sister stations, often appeared and now is on a network show coast-to-coast. I truly enjoyed meeting Arthur Fiedler, David Jansen, John Russell, Joe E. Brown, Vaughn Monroe, Ken Murray, the Victorians, the Kim Sisters, the late Nick Adams, who was a very fine guest, Donald Voorhees, Jack Haskell, Guy Mitchell, the Barry Sisters, and the late Jimmy Dodd, the captivating leader of the Mickey Mouse crowd.

When Kitty Kallen came on the show, she told me that she had not been able to sing in public for several years, due to a nervous condition. However, after we talked a bit, I got her to make a try—and she sang beautifully. When she finished, tears were streaming down her face and the faces of many in the audience.

When the Four Aces appeared on the show, I sang with them my favorite recording of theirs, "Tell Me Why." Dennis Day was greeted by many people who remembered him from the early radio days. I went antique hunting with Joan Blondell. And how we did enjoy Lionel Hampton when he appeared, and the Partners, a singing group who came back many times. The great Jesse Owens also paid us a visit, as did all four brothers of the Crosby family—Dennis, Phil, Lindsay, and Gary. And I was finally able to tell them how much I had always wanted to meet their father.

When Bob Carroll appeared here in the musical *Fiorello,* we had quite a theatre party, and I rode to the theatre in a fire engine. I was later made the first honorary fire chief of

Cincinnati. Later, this same honor was conferred upon Arthur Fiedler of the Boston Symphony, who also loved to attend fires.

The Limelighters, in their very first appearance on our show, were plugging a brand new album. They were completely unknown in this area, having come from the West Coast. They told me they had sold only a few records to date. But we succeeded in selling 80,000 records for them in this area alone. I have since heard that they have broken up the group, which is indeed a real loss to the musical world.

Continuing with our interest in sports, we also invited Mr. Bill DeWitt of the Cincinnati Reds to appear many times on the show, also Mr. Walter Alston, then of the Los Angeles Dodgers, whose home is only about twenty-five miles from Cincinnati. Naturally, one of my favorite people was Waite Hoyt, the former Yankee pitcher, who eventually became a great figure in Cincinnati by doing the baseball reports of the Cincinnati Reds games. Waite and I had been friends since the first day he arrived in Cincinnati, way back at WKRC. He always loved to tease me about "our youth" whenever he was on the show.

In early December, Marian Spelman sang my "Christmas Lullaby" with the Cincinnati Symphony Orchestra at Music Hall. This was a great thrill for me. But the next afternoon I became very ill. And the following day I went to a specialist, who told me I was suffering from complete nervous exhaustion and that I should take two months off and rest. But I couldn't—at this time of the year, and with the Christmas Fund to raise! So after several days at home, I went back to work. I continued to feel very bad day after day, and on December 17, my doctor sent me to the hospital for some tests. All of them pointed to the same diagnosis—nervous exhaustion. On December 21 I was scheduled for my last test. I fought against taking it, for it meant taking an injection of albumin. And how right I was. The moment the injection was put into my arm, I had a dreadful reaction. It cut off the blood supply to my brain, and I was given an angiogram that night. They talked of flying me to Texas for an operation by the famous Dr. DeBakey. But the next day I was much improved. I remained in the hospital for five days, but I had missed the big Christmas show for the first time. I continued to work at home on the Christmas Fund distribution, and a telephone connected with the studio was set up in my home whereby I could telephone into the show whenever I wished to. I had no idea then how long I would use this means of communication. I did not return in person to the "Fifty-Fifty Club" until June 1965, but for an entirely different reason, as I shall tell you later.

chapter nine

The Christmas Fund

It all began in 1939 on a hot summer afternoon, as I have told you, while I was working at WKRC. A number of us had been asked to go over to the Cincinnati Children's Hospital to provide some entertainment for the little patients there. We took several singers, an announcer, and a comedian, all of whom were on the staff. I went along to accompany the singers. As a last minute afterthought we took with us a myna bird, which was supposed to be able to talk. He proved to be quite incommunicado, but the children loved seeing him.

I found Children's Hospital very depressing and sad. It was in a beautiful new building, but inside it was bleak and barren looking. We played and sang for the children and did our best to make them smile a bit, and we all felt very pleased with our endeavors.

It seems that I have always had a mind like a pigeonhole desk, where things get tucked away but eventually come to light at strange times. That year as Christmas time approached, I suddenly began thinking about those little children who would spend Christmas in the hospital. I poured my dismay into the microphone and pleaded with my radio friends to send me a nickel, a dime, or even a penny by a certain date, shortly before Christmas. Some very generous people even sent a dollar, and at the designated time we had $1002. One of our sponsors was Arnold's Fairyland, a toy shop, and I asked them if I might buy at a discount. When they said, "Yes," I was overjoyed.

Since my days at WKRC were so busy and long, the store agreed to stay open overtime so that we might shop at night. $1002 seemed like a million dollars to me. My secretary, Vera Tyson, and I went down to Arnold's and bought dolls, games, cuddly toys, miniature Christmas trees, and books by the dozen. We had gotten a list of the children who would spend Christmas in the hospital, and we bought something for each child according to his or her age. It took us until two o'clock in the morning, and we ended up in our stocking feet! The hospital was delighted when the toys arrived, and we went to see the gifts distributed to the children on Christmas Eve.

One thing I insisted on then and ever since is that I would not permit the purchase of toy soldiers, guns, or armaments of any kind. Later on, cowboy suits and all the appurtenances were permitted as well as Indian headdresses, but that was as far as I would go. After all, cowboys and Indians were a national tradition, which I recall personally with great nostalgia from Custer's Last Stand.

After that first Christmas I told my listeners what great happiness they had given to the hospitalized children, and I began talking about next Christmas and what we would do with their (the listeners') help and generosity.

The second year of the Ruth Lyons' Christmas Fund exceeded all expectations. We raised $10,000. Once more, in our stocking feet, we tried to spend the money for the children in one night, but we couldn't. So we talked with the hospital officials about setting up a fund to be used throughout the year with gifts for the children at Eastertime, Halloween, and for their individual birthdays. Just a small remembrance of ice cream and cake would mean so much. The hospital liked the idea, and it has continued ever since.

Each year the Fund grew, and when in 1942 I left WKRC and went to WLW and WSAI, the Christmas Fund continued. At first we used the facilities of WSAI, and our first year brought in $35,000. One of my biggest thrills was the day I called General Hospital and asked Miss Seymour, a dynamic and lovely person who was in charge of the children's ward at the hospital, if she could use $1000 to buy Christmas gifts for the children in her ward. She nearly dropped the telephone, she told me later, and she handled the Fund from that day on until her retirement several years ago.

So now we had two hospitals sharing in the Christmas Fund! But the best was yet to come. When I started the "Morning Matinee" on WLW, the Fund really began to grow, since WLW's listening area covered so much more territory than we had enjoyed before. So we felt that other hospitals in Indiana and Kentucky, as well as Ohio should be included. We chose the Riley Memorial Hospital in Indianapolis, Indiana, and the Children's Hospital in Louisville, Kentucky, and added them to the two hospitals in the Cincinnati area. We always wanted the money of the Fund to serve the areas from which it came to us. We started Christmas parties at each of the hospitals, and with my enlarged staff we were able to space them all into the Christmas season on various days, usually Saturdays before Christmas.

The General Hospital in Cincinnati was by this time receiving a sizable sum each year, so they built a playroom for the children, which was a dream come true for the indefatigable Miss Seymour. The Cincinnati Children's Hospital, our first, had to build cupboards for storing the toys from the playroom. The hospital in Louisville, which at that time was deplorable, was the saddest of all. Many children from the rural and mountain areas of Kentucky were brought there for treatment, and when we visited the hospital, the existing miserable conditions depressed us greatly.

I shall never forget little Petunia. She was a premature baby who had been abandoned. The doctors and nurses at the hospital had worked day and night to save her, and save her they did! One of the doctors had become so interested in her case and had become so attached to her that eventually he adopted her into his home. I can still see those big blue eyes and that little white face. Another sad case told to me by the nurses was that of a small undernourished little girl who had been found by a case worker. She was lying in bed beside her brother who was dead of starvation. She was being fed every hour at the hospital and was showing progress.

So you can see how much extra money was needed by the hospitals everywhere. This made all the hard work and the long train trips to the hospitals for the Christmas parties, all the more rewarding.

About 1947 WLW bought station WINS in New York City, and our "Morning Matinee" show was carried on the New York station. We made a trip to New York to do the show for a week from the WINS studios, and that Christmas we included a New York hospital in the disbursement of the Christmas Fund. But WLW sold WINS before the next Christmas, so we went back to our original plan of serving Ohio, Indiana, and Kentucky.

In 1950 there was another change made in the raising and the distribution of the Christmas Fund. This was brought about by the fact that our noontime show, the "Fifty-Fifty

Club," went on television and I no longer did the "Morning Matinee" show. This meant that we no longer went into Louisville, but simply drew our contributions from Ohio, northern Kentucky, and Indiana. So some new ideas and revisions were called for. I worried about how the Christmas Fund would fare· that first year on television. Everyone in Ohio, Kentucky, and Indiana could see us worry, as well as hear me threaten daily to "jump off the Suspension Bridge if it failed."

But it didn't fail, nor even falter. That first year on television I wrote a song that is still used every Christmas in raising the Christmas Fund. It was called "Let's Light the Christmas Tree," and that year we raised $39,943.29. What an exciting time it was! And how grateful I was to all the viewers for their support in this endeavor, which was so dear to my heart.

That year after the distribution of the Fund was made to the Children's Hospitals in Cincinnati, Indiana, Columbus, Dayton, and several hospitals in northern Kentucky, we started the idea of the book and toy carts. These carts could be taken from room to room, so the children who were unable to leave their beds and go to the playrooms might select the toys or books they wished to pass the time with. These toy and book carts were replenished daily from the big cupboard where the extra toys were stored. This idea came from one which I practiced in my own home. The generous women who came daily to our television show brought me many, many gifts, fresh vegetables, and their prize jams and jellies, which I took home and kept on my "in-case shelf." "Always prepared" was my motto. When my own little Candy was born and grew older, she was practically inundated with every kind of gift from the viewers, in addition to all that her father and I bought for her. Some of the gifts I sent out to the hospitals, while others which had been made especially for her, I took home and put in a large closet, which she called the "Magic Cupboard." And on days when she was bedded down with a cold or I felt that she was restless and something new would please her, she delighted in receiving something from the "Magic Cupboard." Today, nearly every hospital that is included in the Ruth Lyons' Christmas Fund has a "Candy Newman Magic Cupboard"!

And then we started buying television sets for the hospitals. What a thrill for the children this turned out to be, as well as a great boon to the nurses, who saw to it that the sets were turned on and off, as the children seemed to be quieted by watching the big outside world from which they were shut off. I truly believe that television is the greatest entertainment and comfort, not only for sick children, but also for old people, many who live alone or who are incapacitated. So firmly did I feel about this that I started the Television Fund in addition to the Christmas Fund. From this fund we bought hundreds of television sets for old people's homes, rest homes, and in some cases for a child who was an invalid at home.

Traditionally, the Ruth Lyons' Christmas Fund opened each year on my birthday, October 4, and ran until the week after Christmas. During these three months we observed Christmas every day. By the year 1958 the Fund had grown to $238,272.55, and many more hospitals had been added to the list that shared in it. Many other things were bought besides toys. We provided air conditioning for some hospitals, and we played a large role in the asthmatic respiratory program carried on here in Cincinnati and also air conditioned that building. We equipped a complete kitchen for the girls and a workshop for the boys at our local mental hospital; we bought several station wagons to transport the mentally retarded children on outings to various state fairs; we built outdoor playgrounds at various hospitals; and one very important item which the Fund provided was the rocking chairs we supplied for the mothers to rock their little ones when the mothers had to spend long hours at the hospitals with them.

A most important thing to me was the fact that at no time would I ever show any of the sick children who were at the hospital. I felt that this invaded their privacy and that it was up to me to tell our audience about their many needs without subjecting them to view.

The most wonderful thing about the Ruth Lyons' Christmas Fund is the fact that every cent contributed by the viewers is apportioned to the hospitals each year. WLW hires extra help every year to count the money and tabulate the amount. Some years we had as many as fifteen extra girls working plus all of the girls in my office. Even the singers on the show, as well as the boys in the band, lent a hand. There is a board of directors headed by John T. Murphy, president of Avco Broadcasting Corporation, two well-known doctors, an accountant, the treasurer of Avco, as well as a legal consultant to handle the Fund, which is distributed each year in February after all the donations have been received and tallied. Every year each hospital in the Fund receives a copy of the Aims and Purposes of the Ruth Lyons' Christmas Fund, and every year each hospital must send a report to the committee no later than December 1 in order to be considered in the Fund the following year.

On the "Fifty-Fifty Club" we had a wonderful seven-piece band and four singers, and each year it fell to me to write a new Christmas song for one of the soloists. This helped to create a feeling of freshness to our endeavors. Sometimes I would write that year's Christmas song in June, July, or

August, while on a boat returning from vacation, in a hotel room in New York, and many times while riding in a cab to the studio. I wrote "It's Christmas Time Again" for Bonnie Lou while crossing the Atlantic on the old *Queen Mary*. I wrote the "Christmas Marching Song" on a boat returning from the Caribbean. For dear Ruby Wright the inspiration for "Everywhere the Bells Are Ringing" came while on a trip to Bermuda one hot July day. "Hey Nonny Nonny," a great favorite with the children in our audience, I wrote while under a hair dryer at the beauty salon. Some of the songs I wrote at home, always before going to the studio quite early in the morning, such as the two I wrote for Bob Braun, "Sing a Song of Christmas" and "Only at Christmastime." And there was "Christmas is a Birthday Time," also sung by Ruby, "Soon 'Twill Be Christmas Eve," and "Christmas Lullaby," which Marian Spelman Nimmo sang so beautifully with the Cincinnati Symphony Orchestra. And there was "It's That Happy Time Again," and "This Is Christmas," both written in a cab on my way to the studio. When Peter Grant was on the show I even wrote "All Because It's Christmas" for him. Several others, including "We're Playing Santa Claus," "Once Again It's Christmastime," and "Have a Merry, Merry, Merry, Merry Christmas" were songs in which the studio audience joined in singing. All in all, I wrote more than twenty Christmas songs throughout the years, plus a Thanksgiving song for Marian Spelman.

The gift of writing songs is a gift for which I have always been most grateful. I simply cannot explain it. All at once a tune is running through my head and the words come almost immediately. I never use a piano when composing; I just hear the melody and harmony all at the same time.

To digress for a moment, one evening I was watching a television show on which some of Oscar Hammerstein's lyrics were sung. I turned off the set and went to bed—but not for long. I got up and wrote the song "Wasn't the Summer Short?" in about five minutes. Then I went back to bed and turned on the radio and heard on the eleven o'clock news that Mr. Hammerstein had died a few hours before. Johnny Mathis recorded this song of mine, as did Peter Nero, and both were great successes. I talked about this coincidence the following day to my television audience, as I am sure many of you who read this book will remember.

In 1959, due to the many requests received at the studio by letter and telephone, I decided to record most of my own Christmas songs. This was done in June of that year. Cliff Lash, our band conductor, and Teddy Rakel made some new arrangements to include strings (which our band did not use). With much fear and trepidation, I hired some of the Cincinnati Symphony men—a harpist and another guitarist— and using our own vocalists, with whom the songs were identified, we spent each weekend recording an album called "Ten Tunes of Christmas." I had borrowed some money from WLW to embark on this venture, which I felt was very risky. However, we needn't have worried. We sold over 250,000 albums that Christmas, and I paid all the bills and the remainder was divided equally among all the singers and the members of the band. What a Christmas that was!

As the Fund continued to grow, I felt that we should show our appreciation to the viewers for their continued support. So I decided to have a big Thanksgiving Day show during the regular "Fifty-Fifty Club" hour-and-a-half telecast and a big two-hour long "Holiday Hello" show on the Sunday just before Christmas. The "Holiday Hello" show was the highlight of the year. Ten telephones were installed in the studio from which between seventy and eighty calls were made to viewers whose names were entered in the "Holiday

Hello" file. Then between musical numbers, every member of the cast would man one of the phones and ask the person at the other end of the line a question. If the correct answer was given, and it almost always was, that person received a gift which had been donated to the Christmas Fund. Elsa Sule, who had been with me for more than twenty years, compiled the questions. They were legitimate questions, albeit sometimes farfetched. We had a room where the names of the donors were kept under lock and key, and we would take off our shoes and wade into the thousands of names to make the drawings. And what wonderful gifts we had to give away!

Mr. Karl Gatchett, a dear friend of mine, was greatly interested in the Christmas Fund. He gave a car each year for nineteen years, and for several years he gave us two cars. The Baldwin Piano Company gave us a piano each year. There were color television sets galore, trips to Florida, a trip to Europe, stereos, radios, bicycles for the children, tricycles and dolls for the wee tots, china, silverware, glassware, dishwashers, refrigerators, complete kitchens, and some of the sponsors gave cash in amounts ranging from one hundred to one thousand dollars. In return, we would mention the gifts and their donors during the three months preceding the Christmas show, not every day, but as often as time allowed. We also made a daily telephone call to a viewer or listener. All this in addition to twenty sponsors a day, music, interesting guests, and discussions on everything I felt women were interested in.

One year an incident happened which might have caused us a setback. During his campaign tour of the Midwest, Henry Cabot Lodge, the Republican Vice-Presidential candidate, was invited to appear on the program, as I stated before. A similar invitation was extended to Lyndon B.

Karl Gatchett presents a car to the winner of one of the more than twenty cars he gave to the Ruth Lyons Christmas Fund.

Johnson. The day after Mr. Lodge's appearance, a viewer wrote to me, "You might as well give up on your Christmas Fund. I hope you don't expect any Democrats to donate this year." I was hopping mad, and I read the letter on the air, making the comment, "We have never asked a sick child how his parents vote." The answer seemed to be the turning point in the Christmas Fund that year. Donations swamped the station, and the total reached $316,311.00—the highest ever up to that point. I could not help but quote my favorite proverb, "The Lord will provide." Many of the guests who appeared on the show made considerable contributions to the Christmas Fund to insure its success.

You remember I said the Ruth Lyons' Christmas Fund began in 1939, so in 1968 it was in its twenty-ninth year, being carried on by Bob Braun. Since I retired at the end of the 1966 Fund, this means that I headed the Ruth Lyons' Christmas Fund for twenty-seven years. I received hundreds of awards for this effort. Among these are the first Golden Dome Alumni Award from Notre Dame, the McCall's Golden Mike Award, the Variety Club Humanitarian Award, the Governors' Award from the Academy of Arts and Sciences, the Hadassah Award, the Academy of Medicine Award, the Ohio Valley Druggist Association Award, and one from the Chamber of Commerce of Ohio, and the Association of Hospitals of Ohio, to mention a few.

I treasure these many tokens of appreciation, but I feel that I alone do not deserve them. They belong to that great viewing audience of mine, whose generosity made it possible for us to raise $450,000 in 1965 and $474,000 in 1966. To me the most appealing tokens of appreciation were the many letters I received from the children in the hospitals. One little boy even sent me a penny glued to a piece of paper with a note saying how much he appreciated the Ruth Lyons' Christmas Fund. The parents also were greatly intrigued by the Fund, especially when one of their children was hospitalized. Thus we had a very close relationship with the viewers, which has continued throughout the years.

A verse written by a little patient in one of the ninety-four hospitals which the Ruth Lyons' Christmas Fund now serves seems to best express the Ruth Lyons' Christmas Fund:

What is the Christmas Fund?
The Christmas Fund is happiness for sick little girls and boys.
It gives them happy parties and many pretty toys.
It takes away their nervousness and helps rid them of dread.
It helps them to forget their pain and laugh a bit instead.

by Mary Beth Hahn
Aged 8

chapter ten

Our Travels

The reason I am writing this chapter is not to give an account of all the places I have been, but simply to try to show how I attempted to make all of my visits to faraway places something that my entire audience might experience. They loved to hear about all the places I visited—places that they would probably never see, except through my eyes.

It was the custom for us to spend the holidays after Christmas in New York City. Many a cold winter night found Herman in the large mass of people at Times Square, awaiting the large lighted ball on the Times Building to drop, signaling the arrival of the New Year. Candy and I would watch on television back at the hotel until Herman returned, with all kinds of food from the delicatessen for a late night snack. One Christmas weekend we spent at the Greenbriar, in West Virginia, then went on to Washington, D.C., to visit all the beautiful and historic buildings there, including Mount Vernon and Arlington Cemetery. While we were in Arlington, we witnessed a military funeral. Never shall I forget the sad sound when the bugler played "taps" on that dreary winter's day, as the sound of his bugle echoed and reechoed between the neighboring hills.

After crossing the Atlantic when we went to the Coronation, the desire to travel became the most important factor in the lives of Candy, Herman, and me. So the next year we took off for Hawaii, which we really enjoyed. We visited Los Angeles en route, and returned by way of San Francisco and Las Vegas.

From then on we traveled constantly during my vacations. We went to Bermuda, where we renewed acquaintance with friends we had met on our first trip to London. We spent a month in Florida, where Candy learned to swim and dive. We went to Banff, Lake Louise, and all over western Canada, as well as eastern Canada and Nova Scotia. I loved Quebec, and it made me want to go back to France again. We made several (four in all) trips to New Orleans, and one time we returned to Cincinnati on the *Delta Queen*. I rode up the Mississippi and Ohio Rivers in the captain's wheelhouse, which recalled memories of my grandfather, who for many years was a pilot on the Ohio River, traveling between New Orleans and Pittsburgh.

Then we made four trips to the Caribbean. I recall that on one of them, while walking along the old streets in Caracas, Venezuela, I was so intrigued by Simón Bolívar's home that I walked off a high curb and fell on my "Caracas" in Caracas.

Once more we headed west to Las Vegas, where we met Al Hirt and his entire family, and Sarah Vaughan. I took my niece Linda along with us, and when we arrived in Hollywood we visited Disneyland, the Farmers' Market, Knott's Berry Farm, and many of the movie studios. We came home by way of New Orleans, and that is where I ran into trouble.

We were waiting in the railroad station for our train, when I noticed a Negro woman with a small baby. The baby was crying very hard, so I went over to the mother and asked if the baby was ill. She said, "No, just hungry." I noticed that she was trying to warm a full nursing bottle, rubbing it between her hands.

There was a large brightly lighted soda fountain nearby, and I asked the mother why she didn't have the bottle warmed there. She hung her head and said she wasn't permitted to do so. Grabbing the bottle, I marched over to the soda fountain with it and asked the girl behind the counter to please warm it for me. Hesitantly, she finally did, and I returned it to the mother for her baby. Then everything broke loose! A man came rushing up to me, saying that he was the station superintendent and that I had broken one of the rules of the station. I have never been more furious in my life, and I proceeded to let him know it. I concluded by walking deliberately over to one of the two drinking fountains, the one labeled COLORED, and saying in a loud voice as I turned it on, "Why, this water isn't colored at all. This is false advertising." We almost missed our train, but with the station manager following along behind making all sorts of threats in a loud voice, we made it. Intolerance—that is what is wrong with the world today! Intolerance, bigotry, lack of education, and most of all, inhumanity toward others are all lacking in the American dream. And I fear that this will be so for a long time to come!

Our next trip took us by way of Gibraltar, Casablanca, the Mediterranean Islands, and the Island of Malta, to Naples, Italy. From Naples we drove to Pompeii, which I found very fascinating. This old city, buried for centuries by the eruption of Mount Vesuvius, still shows the layout of the town, and one can even read the inscription, "Cave Canem," or "Beware of the dog." From Naples we drove to Rome, where the son of the Pope's courier met us at the hotel and took us to his home in Vatican City, where he showed us the beautiful Vatican Gardens. The following day he called for us and took us for an audience with His Holiness, the late Pope John XXIII. What a wonderful man he was. I remember his very small feet encased in red velvet slippers and his beautiful hands. Pope John XXIII was the third pope with whom Herman had an audience. Pope Pius XI and Pope Pius XII, the latter Herman having met as Eugenio Cardinal Pacelli in 1934, were the other two papal heads.

And I shall never forget St. Peter's Cathedral. It left me simply speechless. I stood with tears running down my cheeks, in complete awe of its beauty and grandeur. I had bought many rosaries and sacred medals, which the Pope blessed, for all of my friends who are of the Catholic faith. These were greatly appreciated by everyone to whom I gave them upon my return home. Each Christmas the young man who had been raised in Vatican City and who was so charming to us, sends us a Christmas card.

Also, in the hotel in Rome I happened to run into Joseph Welch, who had figured so prominently in the McCarthy trials, which I had watched avidly on television. He was a delightful man, and we spent several hours chatting in the lobby. We visited several marvelous restaurants in Rome and took a moonlight ride by carriage past the Colosseum and along the Tiber.

We left Rome for that jewel of a city, Florence. Then on to Venice, a city of tremendous charm. We rode in gondolas, and spent hours in St. Mark's Square, sitting in the sunshine and listening to the small orchestras that played there each afternoon and Candy fed the countless pigeons. We visited the magnificent Venetian glass shops that lined the Grand Canal, and our luggage grew more bulky each time. I also spent hours in the shops and found six amethyst charms and a pair of earrings to match.

From Venice we took a car to Milan, then on to Genoa, from where we drove along the Amalfi Drive, with its magnificent scenery, to Cannes, where the Film Festival was in progress. I met Van Johnson there and saw Sophia Loren for the first time. Herman and our driver were intrigued by the exceedingly scanty bathing suits all the girls were wearing, but Candy and I spent the day watching the wedding of Princess Margaret and Lord Snowden on television. We had a beautiful suite in the hotel, and I hated to leave. However, the driver was finally able to get us to the station, where we took the overnight train for Paris.

Paris! I had almost forgotten how much I loved Paris. Its magnificent bridges, the marvelous shops, the very air of Paris was different. We went to Versailles, the palace that still holds such a fascination, with its Room of Mirrors, its magnificent gardens, and its historic significance. We visited Mal Maison, the home of Napoleon and Josephine Bonaparte. Once again we rode the *Bateaux Mouche,* went to the Folies-Bergère, the Casino de Paris, to the races at St. Cloud, and visited Notre Dame once more and the ever lovely Sacré Coeur. On returning from a trip to SHAEF, the headquarters of General Eisenhower during the war, we passed the home of that enduringly charming man, Maurice Chevalier. We stood on the Avenue des Champs Elysées and watched General De Gaulle as he marched, proud and straight, up to the Arc de Triomphe. Today I find many things to disagree with him about, but I am sure that he loves France, and he is indeed a striking figure. I made many friends in Paris, and I loved each one of them.

On our next trip we went to Spain and Portugal. I did not care too much for Spain. I found it very dry and dusty and the scenery monotonous, although I did like Madrid and Barcelona. I saw my first bullfight in Málaga, and I met a matador. I think, however, that bullfighting is the cruelest contest of man and beast that I have ever witnessed. There is one place in Spain that I loved; this is Segovia. It is magnificent. It looks like a castle from a fairly tale, rising straight up from the rocks surrounding it. After leaving Spain we took a long tour of southern France, ending up, naturally, in Paris.

We spent the following summer in California. Herman played golf at the famous Pebble Beach, and we visited Yosemite and the great Redwood Forest in Muir Woods, coming home from San Francisco through the Feather River Canyon. Candy had her birthday on the way home, and the Mark Hopkins Hotel had given her a cake large enough to share with everyone in the dining car.

Whenever we left on an extended trip, all of the members of the show accompanied us to the Union Terminal for a great send-off. The boys in the band, the girls in the office, the singers, and a great number of viewers as well, gathered at the train station. I shall never forget when we left the following year for a trip to Russia. More than five thousand persons saw us off at the station, with the band playing and all of the kids carrying signs and waving good-by. When we reached Springfield, Ohio, about eighty miles north of Cincinnati, another large contingent of viewers was waiting at the train station. I got off, and the New York Central waited while I shook hands with hundreds of people in farewell. I believe that everyone thought that I was never coming back.

We crossed to England on the *Queen Elizabeth* and visited Ireland and northern Scotland before we took a boat to Bergen, Norway, where we boarded a small boat called the *Meteor*. This was the first tourist ship that had entered Russian waters since the war. We stopped at Stockholm, Sweden; Copenhagen, Denmark; Helsinki, Finland; and finally, Leningrad, Russia. The night before we arrived in Leningrad, the cruise director, a pessimistic and most obnoxious person, called a meeting after dinner of the 138 persons aboard. He proceeded to outline our trip to Moscow and places of interest in Leningrad. He wound up his speech by telling us to expect the worst! The Russian immigration officers would be very rough, he said, and perhaps we would not be permitted to land at all. Some of the passengers were really frightened. I was seated near the back of the room, growing angrier by the minute. Finally, in complete exasperation, I blurted out, "Then please tell me what the H—— are we doing here?" That ended the meeting in a hurry, as many of the passengers relieved their tensions with laughter. Needless to say, that stupid cruise director and I never spoke to each other again.

There were no problems of any kind whatsoever. The immigration officers were very courteous and very helpful in every way. They spoke perfect English, and smiled as they welcomed us ashore. We stayed in Leningrad for just two days, and then took the Red Arrow Express to Moscow. And what a train the Red Arrow Express is! Women performed the duties of conductors, and women attendants served hot tea and caviar sandwiches to everyone on the train. We had a large compartment with a small table and lamp, a radio, and a very large luggage space completely out of the way. It was more like a small hotel room than a train compartment. If only our railroads here in America could achieve some of the same comforts, perhaps we would still have a great many more trains running. And the Red Arrow is always exactly on time, to the very second! We were told we would arrive in Moscow at eight o'clock, and at eight o'clock on the dot we pulled into the station. We stayed in the Hotel Ukraine. There were people of all nations there. It had only been built for one year, but already the floors were beginning to crumble. However, it was very comfortable, and the food was excellent. Many of the hotel staff were German, so we had little trouble in making ourselves understood. Candy celebrated her fourteenth birthday while we were there, and imagine our surprise when we went down to the dining room that night to find the small band waiting at our table ready to sing a Russian birthday song to her and present her with a large chocolate bar, which we found out later had cost them $2.50 in American money. The children were beautiful, so clean and with huge ribbons in their hair. Everywhere were flowers, which people often bought instead of bread, for the stores were nearly empty of both food and merchandise. Every day we would see long lines of women waiting to be let in to buy a few potatoes, a small watermelon, or a bunch of beets. I saw no meat shops anywhere, but on nearly every street corner you could buy the most marvelous ice cream I have ever tasted.

I visited the huge department store called "Gum's" in English. I bought a few scarves, or "babushkas," as they are called in Russia; a sleazy rayon slip cost $27.50 in American money. I remember one thing that occurred while shopping in Russia. I was looking at some marble statuettes made in the Ural Mountains, when a lovely young woman suddenly touched me on the arm. In excellent English, she told me she was from Kiev, that she was studying at the university there, and that she hoped to become a teacher. She talked for a long time, and I found out that her greatest desire was to come to America. She helped me in the purchase of a marble statue, "Old Man of the Mountain," which resembles our American Santa Claus.

The tremendous network of the Moscow subway is superb. It stretches from east to west, from north to south, and is reached by escalator. Every station was decorated in various themes and brilliantly lighted, and there was an air conditioning system, the efficiency of which I have never experienced before or since. It was not cold, but just like fresh air blowing through the cars and stations. We got off at each station and marveled at the murals, the walls, the sculptured works of art, and above all, the cleanliness of them. We visited the University of Moscow, which was crowded with students—serious-looking young people, the girls with long braids down their backs. We went to a great gathering in the nearby Moscow Stadium, where more than 100,000 people were assembled to view a soccer game and an exhibition of calisthenics (and to have a chance to win a current model of a Russian car!). We also saw the most marvelous "puppet show" with puppets that were life-size. We could not understand a word of the language spoken, but the universal actions of the puppets were quite realistic, and we laughed just as hard as the Russians did. One woman, in unsuppressed enthusiasm, grabbed Herman's arm and they both laughed heartily!

I shall never forget the day we went to Red Square to visit the tombs of Lenin and Stalin (whose remains were still there). We stood for hours in pouring rain. When we finally reached the large marble tomb, which was guarded by soldiers (we saw them change the guard twice while we were waiting in line), we went down, down, down four flights of marble stairs, and it grew colder every step of the day. At the very bottom, there they lay, side by side. They looked like they were asleep, so perfect was the method of embalming employed by the Russians, a secret which has never been revealed. Then we went up, up, up and out into the rain again. Our shoes were soaked as were all of our clothes, but fortunately not one of us caught cold.

I had mixed emotions about Russia. I recall the day we visited the Kremlin Museum to see the marvelous jewels and creations made for the czars by Fabergé, and seeing a peasant man who had brought a small boy to see this storehouse of treasures and precious jewels. They were fascinated and pressed their faces to the glass, which held so much wealth. All of this now belonged to the state, and the people were invited to view it whenever they pleased. Formerly they would not have been permitted anywhere near the czars' treasures.

We returned from Moscow to Leningrad, once again taking the Red Arrow Express. I spent most of the night looking out of the window, where I saw much that reminded me of the old Russia—poorly built homes not much better than hovels; small, barren farms; antiquated farm machinery—all just a few hundred miles from Moscow.

Leningrad was magnificent, with its Winter Palace, its fabulous art museum, and its parks and beautiful buildings along the Neva River. And then we left Russia, and I have since wondered what it is like today. There must be many changes—so much building going on, the Bolshoi Ballet traveling to other countries, the first man-in-space flight, the presence of the nuclear bomb—all of these must have made an impression on the people. I have kept up with many of these changes by reading *Soviet Life*, a splendid journal which is part of the State Department cultural exchange. My daughter became a great student of Russian literature, as did I, but this Eastern World is still an enigma to me, and probably always will be.

Our ship, after leaving Leningrad, docked at Gdynia, Poland, and it was there that one of the most moving experiences of the trip transpired. At the newly constructed docks, British, American, and Polish flags were waved, and the Polish people had hung a large banner which read, *"Welcome American Millionaires."* As each person left the ship, the huge crowd which had gathered applauded each one of us. Poland had suffered dreadfully during the war, as you all know, and this all came home to me as I stood at the rail of the ship.

We took a train to Warsaw, and there I saw what war had really done to a city. They were rebuilding street after street, with each building an exact replica of what had once stood there. Even the very colors were being duplicated. I shall never forget how the tears rolled from the eyes of our guide as he pointed out to us the rebuilding, as we stood in one corner of a cathedral being restored. We drove far out to the countryside and attended a church, where we heard such lovely music being sung and saw an organ of great antiquity, from which gilded angelic figures playing trumpets emerged. We left Poland by way of the Kiel Canal, a trip which lasted an entire day and took us to Hamburg, Germany, from which we took a train to Paris once more, and then home. There has never been a greater homecoming than the one we received both at WLW and by the viewing audience. My husband wrote an article for the university alumnus paper, and I was constantly interviewed by the newspapers and other publications. I told my audience all that I had seen, what I had felt, and that in my opinion communism would never triumph over democracy.

The following year we took a boat to Jamaica, Trinidad, Puerto Rico, and Cuba, where I felt fear for the first time. In Havana, at each store entrance stood one of Castro's men heavily armed. And to add to my fear, I "stole" a white straw belt in Cuba. It was an accident, I assure you. We were shopping for all the people back home, and I was trying on belts for size. I put one on myself, over the belt I was already wearing. We completed our shopping there and hastily grabbed a cab for the hotel, where Fidel Castro was supposed to land on the roof in a helicopter within the hour. I was still wearing two belts, my own and one with a tag attached. Señor Castro did not appear, and we finally gave up. I didn't discover what I had done until I undressed. Thank goodness we left the following day—on the last boat ever to carry a cruise to Cuba.

In 1963 we sailed for Rotterdam and went from there to Hanover, Germany, where we took a train for Berlin. When we reached Berlin, we experienced an incident which was almost tragic. The train, which was to continue on to East Germany, barely stopped. We were compelled to throw our luggage out of the windows and run in order to get off the train. That was the only time that I literally leaped from a moving train. Berlin was draped with American flags, for we arrived two days before the late John F. Kennedy's historic visit. The night we arrived we took a cab, and though it was raining very hard, we rode around near the Brandenburg Gate, where I climbed up onto the reviewing stand, which had been constructed for President Kennedy's visit. There were British soldiers all about, and they gave me permission. Imagine the shock I got the following morning when I went back there and saw Russian soldiers and Russian artillery atop the gate all pointed toward the west. We saw that dreadful wall, covered with broken colored glass embedded in its top and barbed wire above that. All the windows in the houses facing the west had been boarded up, and in the street that ran along the wall we saw flowers and plaques in many places, noting the spots where persons had jumped to their deaths from the windows above. When we went through Checkpoint Charlie into East Berlin, the guards went through all our purses and confiscated any cameras that people might be carrying. I had my traveler's checks under my hat, lest anything untoward should occur. East Berlin was a shambles, all except a large park at the end of the drive, where we were permitted to walk about at leisure. This park was a memorial to the Russian soldiers who had died in the war. There were huge marble statues everywhere and a large marble stairway leading down into the park. Everything was immaculate. We were not permitted to go on any of the side streets, but had to return on the same bus to the checkpoint, where all of our purses were returned with nothing missing. But I did not "tip my hat" in appreciation. We had dinner that night at a beautiful dining room on the outskirts of West Berlin, and we also saw where many of the American officers were living. The next day we left, and this proved to be a nerve-racking experience. You see, we had our passports stamped at Marienbad on the way into Berlin, and we found out we were supposed to leave from the point that we had entered. Not realizing this, we got on the train, and soon four officials came and asked us for our passports. We were riding through East Germany at this time, and we rode for the entire day through East Germany in near panic. Ever so often the Russian officials would come to our compartment and simply stare at us. My daughter went on with her quilting, as she always did while traveling on trains, while Herman and I fumed. At long last, about an hour before we reached Munich, our destination, our passports were returned to us. In Munich I visited the headquarters of Radio Free Europe, and I met the first friendly face I had seen for days. This was a young man from Ohio who headed up the American branch of Radio Free Europe. He, his wife, and little boy were hungry for news of home. We brought them up-to-date on all the news from Ohio, and they were most grateful. There were many American boys stationed in Munich at this time, and I was able to look up a few of them for my viewers back home.

Then by car we drove to Vienna, Austria, with side trips to Salzburg, Berchtesgaden, and Oberammergau, where I met the man who played the role of Christ in the Passion Play which is staged there very four years. In Vienna we had a marvelous hotel, once a palace of Franz Josef. We were permitted by the government to make a twenty-four hour visit to a small town in Hungary. This was very depressing. It was as though we had gone back to a former century to witness the utter backwardness of the cheap market, the old church falling into ruins, and the destitution of the people.

But the worst was still to come. On the outskirts of Vienna was a Second World War camp, Dachau, where thousands of innocent Jews met death by starvation or in the mammoth ovens. Our driver was a former German major in the Luftwaffe, and he begged me not to go to Dachau. But I had to go and see the prime example of man's inhumanity to man. When we got there, the driver did not go in, but paced back and forth along the barbed-wire fence. Inside were displayed clothing of the former prisoners, dreadful pictures of the atrocities that had been committed there, and a small statue of a Jew dressed in prison garb. There was a handful of flowers placed at his feet. A number of tourists were milling about, among them two American soldiers carrying a portable radio, which was blaring music from the Armed Service Radio Station. I shall never forget the shame I felt. Herman went up to them and asked them to respect the shrine of the more than 50,000 Jews who were buried there. They did so, but I still felt that a great sacrilege had been committed.

We went from Vienna to Paris by train. On the train was the London Ballet Company, which had been appearing in Vienna at the magnificent opera house, and having seen the ballet, it was a joy to meet and visit with them. I hope one day to return again to Vienna.

In 1964 and 1965 we spent six weeks in England and Scotland. In 1964 we drove the entire length and breadth of both countries. The following year, 1965, we stayed in London, with side trips to the home of Winston Churchill, his place of burial, and Canterbury.

Then in 1966 came our last trip. Following a visit to Candy's favorite, California, we sailed on June 3, from New York on the S.S. *Michelangelo* for Genoa, Cannes, and Paris. We arrived in Genoa on June 11, where Candy was taken from the ship to a hospital in Genoa. The great compassion of the ship's physicians and the staff at the Internationale Hospital made it possible for Herman and me to be constantly with Candy—day and night. On June 15, we boarded the *Michelangelo* to return home. On June 19, just at sunset, our beloved "little princess" died in the ship's hospital, under the care of Dr. Luigi Guerrini and Dr. Carlo Manfredi. On that saddest of all nights that I shall ever know, I wrote the following:

To My Beloved Candy

On board S.S. *Michelangelo* June 20, 1966

My darling is gone—my love—my heart. Always so understanding—so peacefully companionable—so quick to laugh—so beautifully dignified. So willing to serve in any way—so anxious never to offend. So instinctively honest—so widely versed in all the details of whatever you asked of her. So gentle—so trusting—so loyal to those she loved. So obedient without being servile. So quick to respond to your every wish. So beautiful, with her lovely brown eyes and hair, her peaches and cream complexion, her graceful slim waist. Her long, tapering fingers—so fragile, yet so useful. Her delightful sense of humor—her slow smile of pure delighted pleasure. So tireless whatever she undertook—so fascinated by beautiful things. So unafraid—yet never venturesome. So sensitive to every situation, good or bad. So patient—with her lovely soft voice. She moved in beauty and dignity, and was ever—our "little princess"—so quietly joyous.

And in her father's words—An "unfinished quilt" of uncommon magnificence—our dearly beloved Candy.

chapter eleven

Candy

●━●

I intended to return to the show in February 1965, after a month's recuperation. This was not to be. On January 15, my beloved daughter was hospitalized. The doctor said the surgery would be minor. I paced the floor at home for what seemed an eternity. And then came the dreaded phone call. My beautiful, lovely, darling child had cancer. I nearly collapsed, as did my husband, who had felt all along that Candy's condition was serious.

Words can never express what I felt during the days and the months that followed. Even now I cannot quite accept the fact that Candy, who was so full of joy, so interested in everything, so companionable, should be stricken in this way. She never complained, never felt sorry for herself. Her every thought was for me and her devoted father.

I wanted to retire from WLW, but Candy would not hear of it. She begged me to try to get well enough to return to the show. And naturally, WLW wanted me to come back. They did everything to help me in every way to continue an interest in the "Fifty-Fifty Club." The sponsors grew a bit restive, but they continued on the show, hoping I would be back. A microphone was set up in my home, whereby I could

Candy and I at WLW Studios.

talk to the audience several times a week, and one of my secretaries, Gloria Rush, even brought one of my mike flowers and attached it to the microphone. I continued in this manner until April 9, when I returned to the show. And from the day I returned, Candy went with me every day through Christmas. She was my strength—my inspiration for living. We went to England for four weeks during that summer, and Candy seemed much better. She swam nearly every day, and we both rode our bicycles daily.

In September, Mr. John T. Murphy, who had been wonderful throughout this dreadful year, made Candy a member of the "Fifty-Fifty Club" staff. Candy had practically grown up on the show, and every Christmas had spent her holidays helping with the Christmas Fund. She was a delight to the audience on the show! She worked with Bob Braun and Peter Grant on the two days of the week that I stayed home. She greeted the guests, served them coffee in my office, and they all fell in love with her. She worked on the Christmas Fund on the days I was on the show, but the audience would always ask if she was in my office. When I said she was, they would demand that she come in the studio after the show was over so they could meet her. She loved to do this, and to help the set-up boys give out the gifts to the audience.

In a newspaper interview with Mary Wood of the *Cincinnati Post & Times-Star*, when Candy was asked how she felt about being on the show, she said she loved it. "I went right out and bought a fur coat," she said laughingly. "A fool and her money are soon parted.

"Fortunately, I use most of the products, so I can do the commercials from the standpoint of a consumer." Mary asked Candy what growing up as the daughter of Cincinnati's number one television attraction was like. "I wouldn't know what to expect if I hadn't been Ruth Lyons' daughter," Candy

With Mr. Murphy, on my return to the Fifty-Fifty Club in June 1965.

Candy greets Bob Hope in my office.

Candy officially joined the Fifty-Fifty Club staff in September 1965, when she was twenty.

replied. "I've been with Mother in the spotlight as long as I can remember, and considering everything, I'm very glad that I'm her daughter," she continued. "Poor Mother!" said Candy. "My complete lack of musical talent is a great blow to her. I've tried the flute, the piano, and the violin—that was the worst—and then I got a guitar. I would play in one key and sing in another. We finally sold it, and my family offered up a prayer of thanksgiving.

"My favorite pastimes are cooking and quilting. I quilt like I am eighty-five years old. I am now on my ninth quilt. It is such a relaxing pastime."

I am sure that working at WLW was the happiest time of her life, and I shall be eternally grateful to John T. Murphy for making it possible.

The Christmas Fund was a tremendous success that year, for it reached a total of $450,000. We had our big "Holiday Hello" show, as was customary, but my heart was heavy. For Candy, after the seemingly great recovery she had made, was once more in the hospital and signs were evident that all was far from well. She started the new year, 1966, with the dread disease giving her much pain throughout her frail body. Once more, I was off the show and doing everything possible to help the dear, sweet child and keep her unaware of how really ill she was. A specialist, however, had told her father that it was hopeless, but I didn't know this. We thought a warmer climate might help, so we made a trip to California. And she did seem some better for a few days. When we returned she was busy planning that last trip to the Mediterranean. She loved to travel, especially by ocean liner. She mapped out the entire trip with the help of her dear friend, Mr. Todd of the Provident Bank Travel Department. Every evening she pored over travel folders or typed her cook book, which she hoped to have published.

The Fifty-Fifty Club cast, 1965: Bonnie Lou, Candy, myself, Marian Spelman, Ruby Wright, Bob Braun, Peter Grant, Cliff Lash.

So on June 3, 1966, we sailed on the Italian liner, the S.S. *Michelangelo,* her father and I filled with trepidation. A few happy moments came for her when she attended the captain's reception, in spite of the fact that she was in great pain. But her illness was to prove fatal before the voyage ended.

Candy was always a most contented child, and this trait continued into her last years. She loved to cook, making all kinds of cakes and cookies and was never afraid to try a new recipe. She also loved to sew. She made a number of dresses and made aprons for Pauline and Callie, our housekeepers, but her greatest interest was in making quilts. Her nine quilts were all beautiful and neatly done.

Her love for animals knew no bounds. She became interested in the Japanese spaniel breed. This is a most lovable dog, but not too well known in America. There are several kennels in England, for the story is that Admiral Perry bought two Japanese spaniels from the Emperor of Japan as a gift to Queen Victoria, and in England there are many dog shows featuring them. They are generally white with black ears and markings, and their noses, somewhat pug-like, must match the black markings. Others are red and white or lemon and white. They are very gentle little dogs, and seldom bark.

At one time Candy had eight of these pets, together with an Irish setter, and a large Persian cat with a patch of orange colored hair on its head. She gave them all excellent care. Her favorite was Mitsu—a lemon-and-white female, which she taught to sit up and come to her. She often brought Mitsu to the show and made many tailored costumes for her to wear. We visited two kennels in England, and Candy corresponded regularly with their owners. Also we visited a large kennel in Long Beach, California, from which three of her dogs were obtained. She once had wanted to be a veterinarian, and she would have been an excellent one.

Candy with Tami-San and Mitsu. She was sixteen here.

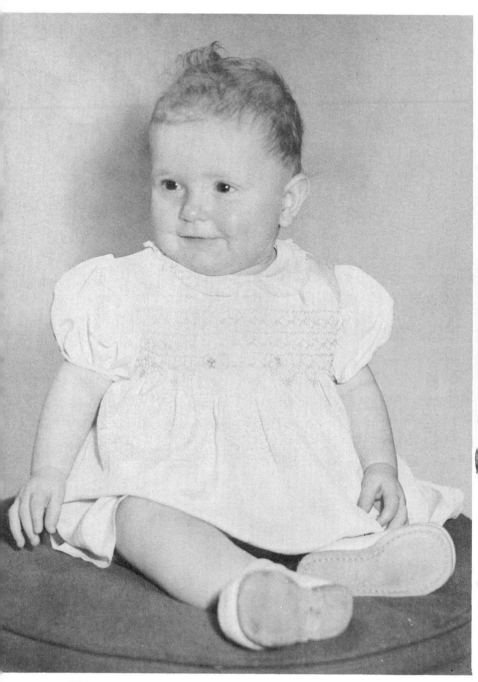

Christmas, 1945. Candy chooses her favorite doll.

Candy at one year.

Wherever we went, Candy always had her quilting pieces with her. She was left-handed, and people were fascinated by the quick movements of her needle. Her great delight was to visit Liberty's fabric department in London and choose from among their countless patterns of material.

She loved the water, and was an excellent swimmer and diver. She had learned to swim when she was three years old, and she entered various swimming tournaments and won a prize for swimming on the *Queen Mary* on one of our trips.

Although not musically inclined, she loved music and knew all the theme songs from the TV shows, which she would sing in her sweet voice while taking her evening shower. Her favorite music was from *The Sound of Music*, which album she played over and over again. We had seen the Broadway production with Mary Martin twice and were fortunate to be able to attend the London premier of the film. Candy loved to read, especially historical biographies. She would browse for hours in book stores looking for books about Queen Victoria, Marie Antoinette, the present-day royal family, and many other monarchs. Her favorite shop for browsing was Foyle's in London, and she carried on quite a correspondence with them. She made a collection of porcelain Japanese spaniels, and once when riding in a cab in Vienna, she saw one in a window from about fifty feet away. We stopped the cab and went back, and sure enough, it was exactly what she said it was.

Candy enjoyed every moment while traveling, and she had many wonderful trips! She never complained or was too tired to go on to visit a castle or a point of interest, or to shop, even when I was ready to drop. I am so glad that she had the opportunity to see as much of the world as she did and meet all the interesting people she met.

Candy could converse readily and easily with anyone. She

Hugh O'Brian visits Cincinnati Children's Hospital with me, Candy and Mitsu.

had a shy little smile, and she never raised her voice. And most delightful of all, she was a perfect listener when someone else was speaking. I am sure this accounted for her retentiveness. Her sense of humor was charming. When she went to a movie that she enjoyed, she would grab hold of my hand, and at a funny episode she would whisper, "Oh, Mother!" and dissolve with laughter.

There are so many things that I remember so vividly, but it is too hard for me to try to write them all.

Candy's death was a tragedy that I will never quite accept. There are the endless little reminders of her: her countless favorite ways of doing things, the songs she loved, the memory of her sweet smile, her charming giggle, her companionship—and most of all, her great consideration of others.

These all add up to the memories that I shall never forget. It was my custom each year when Candy's birthday came, to write little notes of appreciation for her to read when she grew up. Here are some excerpts from several of them:

Moscow, August 27, 1958

You are sitting at a small table. The radio is playing a piano concert. On the table is a strange little lamp which casts your silhouette on the pale green wall behind you. Never have I seen a more beautiful reflection. So quietly beautiful, so sweet and trusting, so utterly beloved! It is moments like this that convince me that no mother has ever been so blessed. What a perfect, lovely companion you are to me. No two mortals have ever known a greater love and understanding than has always been ours.

In two days you will be fourteen years old, on the threshold of becoming the most lovable young lady ever to grace this earth. Each year has only made you more dear to me and to your adoring father, and it is because you are as you are—

Candy at the age of ten.

beautiful and kind in your every thought and action. I want to wish you, dear Candy, a wonderful birthday and to thank you for another wonderful year.

Happy Birthday, beloved Candy,
Mother

P.S. Go to sleep, my darling, and "wake soft," as the Welsh say.

August 27, 1960

Our daughter is now sixteen—taller than I by nearly an inch, round-faced, clear-eyed, with a delicacy of features that grows more lovely day by day. She still runs fast and long-legged, yet her quiet stillnesses are as soothing as a limpid pool. Her gentleness of hands and heart is beyond description. She is happiness personified—without the slightest exaggeration or obvious pretense. Her steady, quiet industry is unflagging. Her duties of sewing, tending to her beloved dogs, bringing in the mail and paper, baking cookies and cakes, are all accomplished without flurry or ostentation. Her concern for my well-being and that of her father is not artificial—it is part of her. She is completely artless. In talking with others, her conversation is intelligent, her memory fabulous. Some strong, warm inner peace pervades her being, and is felt by those around her. Her singing has the sound of youth—full of innocence. Her humor is deep and without a trace of impudence or sophistication. To me, she is love incarnate, a symbol of the beauty that soul and body can achieve, but seldom in this short expanse of a lifetime. One could never tire of her presence, rather, long for it after the shortest absence from it. Her smile, when you tell her you like the cake she has baked, is not one of smug satisfaction, but rather one of pure delight that she has done something for you that pleased you. She has no artifice in her make-up. She glows quietly when she stands tall and gentle in her best dress and high-heeled slippers.

Candy when she was fourteen.

A refreshing oasis, a cool drink of water on a hot day, a warm fireside on a chilly evening, a symbol of outward beauty that shines from within—this is our dear Candy—aged sixteen.

Monday, August 27, 1962
My dear Candy,

Today you are eighteen. And what a wonderful young lady you have become. Nearly an inch taller than I—slender and dainty, grown-up in one way, and yet so young and trusting in many other ways. You are such a delight to be with—quiet, gentle, intelligent, and kind. Your steady devotion to me and your father—your love of your many pets, and the wonderful care you give them—your gentle sense of humor, your beautiful eyes and delicate features—all of these are Candy—aged eighteen.

You love to cook, and you do so very well. Your sewing is perfect, especially the lovely quilts you have made. Your methodical method of keeping house—all of these are not only commendable, but unusual as well, in an eighteen year old today. This will be your last year of high school—then college. I hope you will discover some field in education where you will be happy. I also hope that you will learn shorthand and typing, which I believe are always helpful in getting a job.

You have never been extravagant in spending your money. True, you have not had to earn your way thus far, but should time and circumstances demand that you do, be ready.

Always be friendly, enjoy yourself, but never, no matter how attentive a boy seems, permit him to talk you into anything that you know is not right. You understand right from wrong, and keep holding firm to your own dignity and personality.

No daughter was ever more beloved by both mother and father than you have been, and are at this moment. Today, both your father and I restate that love—and may we both be able to do so for many years to come.

Mother

Candy at nineteen.

Mrs. Alice Kennelly Roberts wrote the following tribute in her column "Rime 'n' Reason," which is published in the *Cincinnati Enquirer*'s Kentucky edition.

In Memory of Miss Candy Newman

There will be songs she loved at every Christmas . . . And dogs and kittens—all her heart could hold . . . There will be laughter and the joy of living . . . Remembering one who never did grow old . . . There will be children watching television . . . Listening for voices on the telephone . . . Hospitals will recall her mother's visits . . . And the brave fight of one so young, alone . . . Courage and faith, and underneath, the heartbreak . . . Tears which the world could never really see . . . These are the background of the poignant story . . . Daughter of one, who gave so generously . . . Yet in so many ways, the name will linger . . . In works her mother did for others here . . . Words are inadequate, assuaging sorrow . . . But in the heart, we'll always hold her dear.

Herman and I received thousands of cards of sympathy from the viewers and friends. The messages contained were beautiful and heart-rending—such as this one: "Candy's gentle smile will long be engraved in all of our hearts."

The reservoir of my tears is bottomless . . .

In October of 1966, because I knew Candy would have wanted it, I went back on the show and raised the Christmas Fund for that year. The total reached $474,000, but the strain was too great, and I left the show. Mr. Walter Bartlett, vice-president of Avco, read this message, my last to all my dear friends in television and radio. It speaks for itself.

January 27, 1967

After being with you daily over 18 years, I will never forget many of you who have done so much for me.

1. First of all the Avco Corporation and all its employees— with a special thank you to Mr. John T. Murphy and Mr. Walter Bartlett for their understanding and consideration and especially their generous support of the Ruth Lyons' Christmas Fund.

2. The many wonderful sponsors who have shown their faith in me year after year.

3. But most especially you, the great audience out there, who, for so long have supported my every endeavor and have written thousands of letters of inspiration and sympathetic understanding to sustain me many times when I needed them so much. And you who have also contributed through the years to the Ruth Lyons' Christmas Fund, my most cherished endeavor.

4. I want to express my love and appreciation to my four girls, Elsa, Mickey, Gloria and Andrea, without whose loyalty and help I would have been unable to continue for as long as I have.

5. To Clifford and those fine boys in the band for all they have contributed to my enjoyment as well as yours.

6. To Bill Gustin, my kind and untiring producer.

7. To the dedicated and talented vocalists, Ruby Wright, Bonnie Lou, Marian Spelman and Coleen Sharp, who have sung so beautifully for all of you, to my great delight, and to the other boys and girls, in their various capacities who have helped to make this show one of which I can ever be proud.

8. To all the fine engineers who have treated me so kindly through the years as good friends.

9. To Mr. Bill McCluskey, "Bonnie Man" whom I have so long admired and relied on.

10. To Peter Grant for his great help, his delightful sense of humor and his true friendship.
11. To Nick Clooney for his youthful enthusiasm and his delightful charm.
12. And to Bob Braun for his unfailing willingness to stand beside me for these past ten years offering encouragement and help, when I know that at many times it must have been difficult for him to do. May I ask that you, the great viewing and listening audience, continue to help and encourage him in every way as you have done for me.

And now I say goodbye, with my love and appreciation for each and every one of you—and I hope that you will never forget as it says in the Second Book of Timothy—"I have fought a good fight—I have run my course—I have kept the faith!"

Sincerely,
Ruth Lyons

After my retirement, I received thousands of beautiful letters from my former viewers and listeners. I read them all, and they convinced me that my daily shows had meant very much to them. From dear old ladies, from children, from young mothers and housewives, from men in all walks of life, they flowed in. To quote from a few:

Dear Ruth,

I began watching your show when I was in college ten years ago. I believe that what I enjoyed most was the fact that you are a thinking person, and that you make other people think.

Now my two little girls will miss seeing you. But we believe in the great good the Christmas Fund has achieved, and we shall continue to support it in memory of you and Candy.

I want you to know how privileged I have been to have been able to watch, learn, laugh, and cry with you, and what an honor it has been to 'know' you.

My dear Ruth,
   Twenty years ago this June if anyone would have told me that I would have latched onto a radio personality and listened religiously ever since, and later watched on television, and break down and sob when she retired, I wouldn't have believed it possible. Nothing will ever erase you, Herman, and your beloved Candy from our memory.

Dear Miss Lyons,
   When you sang 'Let Me Entertain You' day after day, you did exactly that. No television star or anyone connected with show business has ever become such a close friend to so many as you have. You introduced us to so many great guest stars, and helped us to know them better. You brought us beautiful songs, songs which you wrote from your heart. You made us feel important, and to try to be more thoughtful and considerate of others. Now please, please write a book for us all to cherish in years to come.

A tree was planted in Israel in memory of Candy, and a beautiful stained-glass window was given by Riley Memorial Hospital in Indianapolis in tribute to her. It shows a little girl sweeping and was modeled after a Hummel figurine, a copy of which stands on the table beneath her picture in our home.

So you see, the world is still full of kindness, sympathy, and thoughtfulness, even in this year of tragedy, war, racial hatred, and world crises.

chapter twelve

What Others Have to Say

In writing a book that covers nearly a lifetime, it is difficult to talk about oneself. Here are some expressions of recollection and esteem written by my dear friends, Elsa Sule, who was with me for twenty-two years; by Mary Wood, the TV columnist for the *Cincinnati Post* & *Times-Star;* by Mickey Fisher, who served so well as my private secretary for more than ten years; and by Gloria Rush, a very dear friend who worked for me, and who, since my retirement, has been of great help and consolation. As you read what they wrote, remember that they all wrote spontaneously, and I truly appreciate their fine tributes.

First, from Elsa Sule:

I, by dint of sheer longevity, wanted to write a verbal portrait of Ruth Lyons—as she looks to one of the "girls" (and I use that term loosely!) in the office.

When someone came to work on Miss Lyons' staff, they stayed—usually for at least from ten to twenty years! Listeners and viewers came to know the office staff as well as the talent staff—we were "a family." Well known and well remembered are Vera Tyson, Miss Lyons' secretary at WKRC who came to WLW with her; Sue Bressler West, now married and very happy; Gloria Rush, who retired from television when "Mother" did (Gloria now runs an antique shop); Mickey Fisher, now an executive secretary in the Minneapolis area, where her husband was transferred; Andy Sams (always called "Sandy" by Miss L—for no particular reason), now wife of 1st Lt. William McCay.

Around these parts, it's said that if Ruth Lyons walked down the street with the President of the United States, any woman nearby would nudge her companion and say, "Who's that man with 'Mother?' He doesn't look like Herman." Be the lady seventeen or eighty-seven, Ruth Lyons to her would be easily recognizable, known as "Mother"—and "Mother" shouldn't be running around with anyone other than Herman.

The name "Mother" stemmed not from any personal relationships nor even from any comparative ages. I guess it came into being because Ruth Lyons played parent to all co-workers, as well as to listeners and viewers. When anyone was in a scrape of any variety, "Mother" Lyons came to the rescue—whether it required patching up a lovers' quarrel or saving a job. She could always be counted on to make the old college try when the cause was just. Justice has always been her fetish. And she was effective. This I know from personal experience.

"Mother" saved people's jobs for a number of reasons. In radio and television, as, I'm sure, in other businesses, there are periodic economy waves. Those elected to go are selected for various and sundry reasons—ability usually being one of the lesser determining factors—and this brought "Mother's" fighting blood to the boiling point. In one instance—after much deliberation—the finger was pointed at one of the musicians, a man we all adored, but one who could be eliminated without too many changes in arrangements. Miss L had been in on the conferences, and although she didn't approve, there didn't seem to be any other solution, so she was going along. This passiveness lasted only till one afternoon when "Mother" and I were in the main lobby waiting for a cab and said musician walked through. She took one look at him, and said, "Those poor, dear flat feet—he can't go!" She marched straight to the office of the president of the company—and WLW rehired him.

Walking down a street in New York with Miss L was never too different from walking down one in Cincinnati. One spring she and I went to the "big city" with a sales presentation for the New York office. By merest chance, we wound up with time to see a few shows—merest chance and careful design! On Wednesday afternoon we journeyed to the matinee of *Fiorello*—and loved it.

After the performance, we gave up on the cab situation and were strolling toward the hotel when a joyful cry of "Mother!" penetrated the air. We turned to see a most attractive young lady in leopard coat, sun glasses and complete stage make-up. On second glance, we recognized her as Pat Wilson, the girl who played the lead in the show. What we didn't know until two minutes later was that Pat Wilson had grown up in Cincinnati—with "Mother" Lyons on the radio and TV set—and was overjoyed to find her "almost-relative" in New York. The two chatted gaily, signed autographs—and I hummed "There's No Place Like Home" under my breath.

The same evening Miss Lyons and I went to weep over *Sound of Music*. We always cry at shows—if they're good— be they comedy or tragedy. There's always something touching and beautiful, and besides, "Mother" cries at the drop of a handkerchief, and when she does, I do. It was a great show, and "Mother" got so carried away that she forgot her gloves.

I left her by the stage-door and went back to retrieve them. The gloves were easily found, and as I approached the spot where I'd left her, I heard another joyful yelp of "Mother!" This time it came from Brian Davies, who was playing the juvenile lead in the show. He had been a guest on "Mother's" program a number of times, and besides, he'd lived in Indianapolis. Again, a great reunion followed. Brian took us back-stage, and we met all the lovely people in the cast. We both adored Mary Martin, and she and I had a marvelous chat about how to put in contact lenses.

There was always instant empathy between Miss L and the guests on her show—probably a major reason why she was such a successful interviewer. She was interested in the guests—as people and human beings to be admired for their talents—and she listened to their answers to her questions. Once when Denise Darcel came on the show, she looked like the typical, glamorous movie star when she entered the scene. A few minutes later, she spied a little lady in the second row who reminded her of her mother. The tears began to flow. Miss L immediately joined in. The audience most assuredly did not want to be left out—and shortly thereafter we were rowing around the studio in boats. It was a lovely interview—and Mademoiselle Darcel was a soggy mess when it ended.

Miss L is probably the greatest game player I've ever known. She is a fierce competitor and plays to win. We've had beautiful "discussions" about the interpretation of the rules of everything we've ever played, and she wins those, too. She's marvelous at all sorts of word games, and she's a wonderful partner at bridge (in spite of that blasted short club!). We used to spend our lunch hours with a deck of cards, and despite the fact that it was "time off," more decisions were made quickly and decisively then than at any other time. Bill McCluskey, "Mother's" favorite partner (other than me—or Mickey—or Gloria) came to join us, and business was transacted between hands with amazing alacrity and efficiency.

As the world knows, Ruth Lyons was one of radio and television's most successful "salesmen." Sponsors waited for years to get on her show, and when they did and she endorsed their product, they were "made" in the Midwest. She would never, however, endorse a product until she was personally convinced that it was the best in its field. She conducted—personally—endless tests on everything that came on the program, and viewers and listeners came, thereby, to depend on her word. She was the same way about premium offers. If she did not feel they were a real value, off they went—even if the account went along. In meetings she never minced words with sponsors or agency men. She told them exactly how she felt about their wares and their campaigns, and they respected her for it. They also realized that several million women would feel the same way—and what mere man is going to argue with several million women—or one named Ruth Lyons?

Although Ruth Lyons has been off the air since January 27, 1967, everywhere I go I'm asked one question—"How's Mother?" The girls who clerk in the stores want to know—as do the people who go to our church, friends at cocktail parties, truck drivers who call from their trucks (wish they'd whistle, too!) and former co-workers here at the station. Here at WLW it's the engineers who inquire most often—but the musicians and the maintenance men aren't far behind. And a charming and respected retired English professor at the University wanted to know about "Mother" the other week.

Listeners and viewers, and even co-workers, have in the

past and even more now a tendency to beatify Ruth Lyons in her own time. In spite of her wonderful works, this is a lot of nonsense! She's far too much of a human being—and far too much fun to be with. Maybe saints have senses of humor, but not like hers! Besides, no saint would ever:

1. Write a heavenly song—in a taxi on the way to work—and hand Cliff Lash, on the air, two notes scrawled on the back of an envelope and say, "Play this!"
2. Compose delightful, singable lyrics every second grader in a three-state area can reel off without a moment's hesitation—and not remember one word of them herself—without a large "idiot" sheet.
3. Have a built-in sense of timing and be able to do an ad lib 60-second commercial in exactly 60 seconds—and still be late on her show four days out of five—because she was so involved in something she forgot to come into the studio.
4. "Grandstand manage" the Cincinnati Reds and the University of Cincinnati Basketball Team—but feel that wearing a decorated, lucky hat during a game is much more strategy than superstition.
5. Adore her husband and be sentimental to the hilt—and invariably ask, "Elsa, when was I married?"

A saint wouldn't, but Ruth Lyons would and does—and that's why she's Ruth "Mother" Lyons, more than a Boss-Lady, a really incomparable friend!

Next, from Mary Wood:

That January day, in 1967, when Ruth Lyons announced her retirement, was a bleak day for thousands of people who had watched Ruth's "Fifty-Fifty Club" for years and considered her a loved and important member of their family.

She was never a TV-radio personality to her fans. She was "Ruth" or "Mother" and she was their dear friend.

How often has one of them asked me that familiar question: "You and Ruth have been friends for such a long time. What is she really like?"

Well, Ruth can't be described in a few words because she's totally female and a lot smarter than most. She's sentimental, funny, lacrimose, gay, sad, tender and tough at different times. She's stubborn, argumentative, inquisitive, courageous and opinionated at different times. In other words, she's a woman and, in my opinion, a great one. We laughed together, cried together and, at times, fought like Kilkenny cats over something or other.

Ruth has had me in her corner since we first met when she came to WLW over twenty-five years ago. I suppose it was her terrific sense of humor that hooked me and here's how it happened:

Ruth had just joined WLW from another Cincinnati station, WKRC, and, like any other newcomer, she was carefully inspected by the other females at WLW, including me. We were sitting in the cafeteria one morning, drinking coffee and discussing Ruth when she breezed in and sat down with the astonished group. There was a brief, stricken silence, which Ruth broke almost at once.

"Well," she asked, "have you decided whether or not you like me?"

Now who could resist such an honest approach. She was in like Flynn.

If anyone asked me to pin-point the reasons for Ruth's tremendous popularity on radio and TV, I could only say that her audience loved her because she was honest, outspoken, warm and funny. She also brought something else into their lives. She made them think. She was a great showman who genuinely liked and respected her audience—and loved to kid them and herself. She had the rare ability to share jokes, ideas and experiences with them, and they appreciated being treated as intelligent human beings. Her show was a sort of "One Woman's Family" that went on and on for years, becoming more popular each year.

During her more than thirty years on the air—radio, and later, television—Ruth's popularity was legendary throughout broadcasting. Her appeal as a daytime personality has never been equaled, and her ability to sell products was asstonishing.

Although Ruth enjoyed much success in radio, it wasn't until television came along that she really bloomed. They were made for each other. While everyone else in the broadcasting business was struggling to find an approach to this monster infant which was thrust upon them, Ruth knew instinctively what to do. To her, television was a means of getting closer to her audience and to make them a part of her program.

All the network "talk" programs we have today—Johnny Carson, Joey Bishop, Merv Griffin and Mike Douglas—really began when Ruth threw out all the rules for television and "played it by ear." Nothing was rehearsed and she wouldn't even read a script if there had ever been a script to read. To the millions of viewers who tuned in regularly each weekday at noon, and to the thousands who came in bus loads to the studio, Ruth was having a party.

I can't begin to recount the number of celebrities and show business "greats" who have visited "Fifty-Fifty Club" and gone away filled with wonder and admiration at the small, dynamic blonde who had kept a free-wheeling, unrehearsed, ad lib TV program going for ninety minutes without a dull or lagging moment.

"I don't believe it," Milton Berle once told me. "I simply don't believe it. How does she do it?"

That, of course, is the multi-million dollar question, because that is what Ruth Lyons was worth to Avco Broadcasting over the years.

No story about Ruth could fail to mention her Christmas Fund which contributed millions of dollars to hospitals and institutions in Ohio, Kentucky and Indiana to provide entertainment and diversion for sick or convalescent children. It was Ruth's love of children and her tireless devotion to the Fund which made it the great success it became.

Often, I think, the measure of a person is the devotion of the people who work with him. The Fifty-Fifty Club "family," including the boys in Cliff Lash's band, loved "Mother." I used to call her "The Wailing Wall" for WLW-T because everyone came to Ruth with their problems.

I remember a time, years ago, when the Musicians Union was involved in a contract dispute with the management and there was a possibility of a strike until Ruth settled the matter with a memo to the management. She reminded them that she was a member of the union and would therefore be the first in the picket line.

The greatest tragedy in any parent's life is to lose a beloved child, and that is the sorrow Ruth suffered when her darling daughter, Candy, her only child, died of cancer at 21. I know that she will never stop missing Candy and grieving for her, but perhaps, writing this book will help her.

I know that Ruth's countless TV friends still miss their daily visits with "Mother." She was so much a part of their lives for so many years and shared so much with them—her humor, her enthusiasms, her always forthright opinions, her interest and her family. She reached out and touched so many people in so many ways and often made them think while she was entertaining them. Ruth really loved her audience, which is why they responded to her. She made them know that they were important to her, which they were.

Then from Mickey Fisher:

I know it was fate that took me to the studios of WLW Radio and Television on that hot afternoon in August 1957. I went there to apply for a position in the stenographers' pool that had been advertised in the local newspaper. After looking over my application, they asked me if I would like to be interviewed for the stenographic position recently vacated in Ruth Lyons' office. Well, since I had heard of Ruth Lyons since I was knee-high to a grasshopper, having a mother who was a devoted fan of the show for many years, I immediately said, "Yes, I'd love to!"

The interview was handled by Elsa, and I was given two letters to transcribe and Elsa told me she would get in touch with me in the next day or two. I was disappointed at not having the opportunity to meet Ruth Lyons, but I left with my fingers crossed that I would get the job. A day or so later Elsa called and told me to report to work on August 26. I was elated. Thus began the ten most memorable, fun-filled, heart-rending years of my life with the FIRST LADY OF TELEVISION—RUTH LYONS.

To say "to know her is to love her" is a misnomer, as there are thousands and thousands of viewers and listeners who loved her, but never had the opportunity to know her personally. However, to be with and work alongside this lady who had endeared herself to so many was an education in itself.

Within two years I became her personal secretary and confidante. Only once in ten years were there any words between us—a personal problem of my own—and I must admit that she was right and I was wrong as it turned out. "Mother" as she is known to all her co-workers, is the most humane person I have ever known, evidenced by the Christmas Fund, which she raised for 25 years for hospitalized children throughout the tri-state area. The Christmas Fund has continued since her retirement in her name, for it will always be the Ruth Lyons' Christmas Fund in the hearts and minds of the millions of contributors, and the thousands upon thousands of children who benefited from the Fund for 27 years.

How many times I have been asked, "WHAT'S RUTH LYONS REALLY LIKE?"

First of all, Ruth Lyons is real. There is absolutely nothing phony about her. She is honest, opinionated, and expressed her opinion on the air, many times to the sorrow of the station management.

I believe that Ruth's success was due mainly to her outlook on her position as the star of the "Fifty-Fifty Club." I have heard her say so many times that "you never talk down to an audience, because somewhere sitting out there are many people much smarter than you." When you were with Ruth, you had the feeling that you could just sit down and talk as you would with a neighbor or one of the family. How else could you describe her when the audience would bring her vegetables from their gardens, prized jams and jellies, secret cake recipes, fresh eggs, and home-made bread. When they came to see the "Fifty-Fifty Club," it was like visiting with one of the family.

Many times after the program, I have seen a woman from the audience run up to Ruth with tears of adoration in her eyes, who just wanted to shake her hand. Ruth could cry at the drop of a hat, and I have seen tears well up in Ruth's eyes on many of these occasions. I have seen many cry upon Ruth's entrance to the studio at the beginning of the program. Knowing the devotion of so many of her viewers, she was never once dishonest about a product she ever talked about on the program. Only Ruth could approve a product for the program, and it was tested and used in her home before it ever made an appearance on the show.

I will always believe that the client meetings were never for any other purpose than for the visiting clients to just sit down and talk to Ruth—not about the products—just to talk to Ruth. One I recall with a chuckle. It was with the Ball Brothers people. Ruth had advertised Ball Brothers Jars for years and years. They had developed a new lid and wanted to come down and visit Ruth and discuss their promotion on the new product. After the show, Ruth walked into the office, and sitting on the floor of her office were cases and cases of Ball Brothers Jars. Three or four men from the company and the advertising agency were there. Ruth had recently returned from Europe, and they began discussing her trip and her feelings about the anti-Americanism in the countries she had visited. The men came and went without one single word said about the new lids and jars. We laughed the rest of the afternoon about it. Needless to say, the fact sheets left with Ruth were enough for her to sell the products to her audience.

All she ever wanted from the advertising agencies were the facts about the product. She possessed an uncanny memory bank in that blonde head of hers. She had the faculty to be reading one thing, having someone talking to her at the same time, and know exactly what the person said and exactly what she had read.

Ruth's power as a saleswoman is typified by a comment I recall being made on the air by members of the studio audience. On one occasion, a young woman from the audience who was expounding on one of the products advertised on the show, stopped in the middle of what she was saying and asked Ruth if she could tell her what her husband had told her. Ruth, of course, said yes. To which the young lady replied, "My husband said that if they bagged manure and Ruth Lyons sold it for a deodorant, you'd buy it!" It broke up the show and Ruth. The lady never did finish her spiel on the product she was originally talking about.

In my ten years with "Mother" I met many, many celebrities. You might be interested to know that my observation was that the bigger the star, the nicer the person. You normally wouldn't think this, but it's true—at least of the majority I met. As Ruth's personal secretary I had the pleasure of many happy hours of conversation with Ruth and her visiting guests in her warm and lovely office. Those meeting Ruth for the first time never failed to comment about Ruth's ability to bring out the best in them and the way she so quickly put them at ease.

Whenever we wanted Ruth to get onto some controversial subject that had been discussed in the office or was in the news, all we had to say was, "Don't say anything on the air about it." She would leave the office, heading for the studio, promising that she wouldn't say a word, and upon greeting the audience would go right into the subject she promised not to mention. Of course, since it was a controversial subject, the mail would pour in and the phones would ring for days with irate listeners and those who agreed with Ruth. She always spoke her piece, whether on the side of the majority or the minority.

Her relationship with her co-workers was one of true friendship and mother-confessor. Whenever one of the cast or crew had a problem, they took it to "Mother" for her sage advice. She was a good listener and always had time to see any one of them that asked to see her. She is the type of person that you feel you can never quite do enough for—not that she expected it, but because you wanted to.

Once you became a member of the Ruth Lyons TV family, you just never had the desire to be anything else. It really was a family relationship. Even though our offices were in a big building, we always felt that they were an entity all to themselves. Lunch hours were spent in Ruth's office playing bridge with Ruth, Elsa, Gloria and Rose, Ruth's sister, when she was living. The games sometimes ran into more than an hour, but when you're playing bridge with your boss, who's to complain? We would pretend we were famous bridge players—Ruth was always Charlie Goren, and one of us would be Alfred Sheinwald and a couple of other famous experts. Ruth would sip her coke or hot chocolate, while the rest of us ate the display products from the show that day. Ruth never ate any lunch. She always had a late breakfast and an early dinner. For her 29 years she certainly stayed trim following this diet. Quite frankly, even as personal secretary, I never knew her true age. She was always 29 to me, and she shall always be 29.

Ruth is a very generous person. Of course, being on television, she had to have lots of clothes, which she did. Her clothes closet was a small room filled with five or sick racks of clothing. She would periodically go through the closet and discard the dresses, suits, slacks, purses, shoes, etc. that she no longer wanted. It was like Christmastime when she would have them brought down to the studio and we would all go into her office and try them on and take our choice of what we wanted. I was luckier than most, as I fitted into more of them than any of the other girls. Lucky me! This is typical of her generosity. Hardly any of my earnings were spent on clothing in the ten years I was with her.

We had a standing joke around the office about my big feet—that's the only place I was bigger than Ruth. It all started one day when she kiddingly said that if I couldn't wear the shoes, I could wear the boxes they came in and one time jokingly made the comment on the air. Shortly thereafter, I was in a supermarket and I noticed this lady staring at my feet, and when she saw me looking at her she said, "Mickey, your feet aren't that big." We both had a good laugh and discussed Ruth and the show at great length.

Each day was always a new adventure. Things were never dull or routine in the "Lyons Den," as our offices were affectionately called. The mornings were spent in preparation for the program: band rehearsal, product preparation, studio set-up. Since the twenty commercials a day were strictly ad lib, Ruth never needed anything but a rundown of any special promotion involving the products of the day. She would arrive at approximately 11:30 and stroll through my office leaving the scent of Chantilly, her favorite perfume, in her wake. She would glance over the rundown, and this was the total of her preparation for the telecast. Whatever happened on the show just happened. She had a fantastic timing ability and knew just when to throw in a commercial, a musical number or get involved in a controversy.

There was always a waiting list of sponsors to take over whenever a product left the show. Some of the sponsors even requested rebates when Ruth was on vacation or missed a show, as they felt they weren't getting "the real thing"—Ruth Lyons' Stamp of Approval. They wanted Ruth to do the "pitch" and no one else. Of course, they were never given a rebate, but nevertheless the request speaks for itself—it was Ruth Lyons they were buying, and no one else would do.

Who will ever forget the "great cranberry scare" back in

the early sixties. It affected the entire country except in Ruth Lyons land. She talked about Herman having fresh cranberries for dinner and the fact that the story was blown entirely out of proportion. The sales of cranberry products never dropped an iota in the area covered by the show. In fact, sales went up during this period. A letter of thanks and appreciation was sent to Ruth from the Cranberry Association for her staunch support during the crisis.

I recall another incident when it worked in reverse. A gelatin sponsor came out with a new flavor sensation—Watermelon. Ruth didn't think it tasted like watermelon and made no bones about it on the air. Sales of the product went down, and the sponsor finally dropped the flavor from the line.

Life as a member of the "Fifty-Fifty Club" crew was never dull. In the years to come, memories of events during this period of my life will pop up when I least expect them to. There will always be something that will remind me of a certain incident, or a star will appear on television that I have met and I will recall that meeting and smile.

Though a star, Ruth was definitely a wife and mother first. Her daughter Candy was the light of her life. This light was to be forever dimmed when Candy was taken into the arms of God at the age of 21. Their life was strictly the three of them, Ruth—Herman—and Candy. They shared everything and did everything together.

Candy was not the typical child of a star. She was tutored at home throughout most of her school age years due to the cruel remarks of children. We all know how children can sometimes unknowingly say something that hurts. Being the daughter of the very controversial Ruth Lyons was not easy. However, Candy remained sweet and gentle throughout her short life. How many times I have heard Ruth tell about taking Candy downtown to buy some new things and Candy had refused to buy something she really liked, because she felt it cost too much, knowing very well they could afford it. This was Candy. Or when grocery shopping, she would never purchase a product competitive to anything her mother sold on the show. Her own words were, "Mother, what if someone saw me!" She was always thinking of the comfort of her mother and father, fixing her father's favorite cakes and cookies and helping her mother whenever she could.

When she lost Candy, Ruth lost interest in everything. She no longer had the desire to do the show, nor write music, travel or any of the things they shared when there were three of them. I must include Herman at this point, as he was a devoted father to Candy.

I shall never forget the day Ruth called and asked me what she should do with Candy's clothes. She finally decided to give them to an orphanage. Gloria Rush and I went out to Ruth's to pick them up and deliver them to the orphanage. I can't put into words the traumatic experience it was for Gloria and me. Loving Ruth the way we did and to see how brokenhearted she was when we arrived was almost too much to bear. We tried to console her as much as we could, but each dress she took from the closet I could see Candy in it and I know Ruth could. Now that I recall it again, I don't see how Ruth, being half ill herself, went through the ordeal.

Ruth did return to the show, but strictly for one reason—to raise the 1966 Christmas Fund in memory of Candy. Naturally, the Fund was a huge success, raising over $485,000 in two months. After the Fund was raised and allocated, Ruth had no desire to continue with the program. Her decision to retire was made before she ever returned to raise the Fund—none of us knew, but Ruth did. This had been her plan all along.

Just thinking about it now brings tears to my eyes and a

lump in my throat. This was the end of an era, the end of a career that touched the lives of thousands, the end to the dinnertime conversations of the happenings on the Ruth Lyons show, the end of the "Fabulous Ruth Lyons Fifty-Fifty Club." GONE, BUT NEVER TO BE FORGOTTEN.

And last, but not least, from Gloria Rush:

On only two other occasions have I had the opportunity to speak out publicly about Ruth Lyons—to tell of the honor and privilege it was to work for her and to work with her in the exciting world of her kind of show business, but most of all, to sit at her side, to learn from her, to laugh and cry with her, to think with her, and to be honored by others just to be at her side. As Ruth always gave her best to us, we always did our best for her. It seemed we were always to come up to our highest level of ability when we were doing something for her, and I think this was true, not only of us in the office, but of the entire cast of the "Fifty-Fifty Club."

I shall never forget the day Ruth called and asked me to come and work full-time for her. I felt I should ask my husband if it would be all right with him if I worked every day; but then nobody could have stopped me, so I gave Ruth a big "yes" even before she finished the question. I had already been working on the Ruth Lyons' Christmas Fund and ticket sales for several years, and knew of the excitement and fun that prevailed in the "Lyons Den." And now I was part of that wonderful den!

It didn't take me very long to find out that Ruth rarely sent for any of her secretaries. She didn't have to—they always surrounded her. Somehow, like electricity in the air, everyone knew Ruth was there. Whether it was her heavenly Chantilly perfume, or simply vibrations, we all knew that

Ruth had arrived. One by one we came with our notes and messages, all so important, but always Ruth was so bubbling with such interesting things to tell us, and there were many world-shaking problems that we tried to settle before we got to the job at hand. Ruth had the amazing ability to read copy or letters and listen to us at the same time. She did everything spontaneously, and this was, of course, part of her great success. There was always great excitement in the office, and after something quite controversial was discussed, we always made Ruth promise she would stay away from that subject—but she never could. If the studio audience saw us holding our heads or hanging onto the walls, they probably knew we were in for hundreds of letters and phone calls, but now I'd be willing to take a thousand letters and phone calls if I could see Ruth on that couch with her microphone of flowers again.

I have never ceased to be amazed at the strong love and devotion the people have for Ruth Lyons. It is rather unbelievable when you realize that Ruth knew none of these people, and yet they idolized her. How do I know this? Because I read hundreds of thousands of letters to her and took thousands of phone calls to her and about her. The love that flowed out in most cases was beautiful and many times brought tears to my eyes. I learned very early that the Midwestern housewife was capable of good writing. Many times the letters were in pencil or on tablet paper, but written with the quality of an Elizabeth Barrett Browning or a Fannie Hurst. Ruth's fans were anything but stupid, and perhaps they learned much from Ruth. I know that I did, especially after I joined her staff. Sitting at her elbow each day, I learned much about television, advertising, religion, politics (I had much to teach on this subject, but no one ever listened to me), and particularly, I learned about life. We all had refresher courses in spelling and semantics without really knowing that we were getting them. Ruth was such a stickler for perfect spelling, and we could never trap her on any word, but we all made mistakes at one time or another. I think the biggest was the spelling of "rot" iron.

Ruth always had the greatest success with her records. When she was thinking of putting out a third album, we begged her to do one by herself playing the organ, not only because her fans were continually requesting it and we knew it would be a great financial success for her, but because we wanted it for ourselves. But Ruth would not consent. She said, "No, I want to include my entire cast in any record I do." This was meant to be a compliment to her cast, but to me it was another example of her unselfishness.

Many, many of her fans wanted Ruth to put her "I Love Paris" on record, but she would never do this. Her singing was always a big joke to her, but to those devoted thousands it was the high light of any show. They simply thought Ruth should do "I Love Paris" every day. When she was talked into doing it, you could just feel the stirring of the audience in the studio. Everyone sat up to see her every movement, not only the audience, but we too wanted a full view—the master showman was at it again. Of course, this was the time for the set-up boys to get something to drop to interrupt the song. They loved to tease Ruth because they loved her. It was ironic that no matter how many set-up boys Ruth had, and they were always changing because this was a temporary step to something better, and no matter how short their tenure, they all adored this woman. They loved to meet her in the hall with their latest joke, they loved to talk about her to the other boys, and they loved to tell their friends on the outside what Ruth Lyons was really like.

After the show was over, many times the guests stayed

on for a chat with Ruth, but as soon as they left, once again we surrounded Ruth, and if the show had been a great one, and it usually was, the show in the office was even better. Ruth's office was away from everything, very serene, and there was Ruth on her love seat and we girls around her. The stacks of mail to do were usually very high, and as we each got our own letters to write, we would moan and groan about all of Ruth's fan mail, but we really loved every minute of it. She was always very easy with us, never demanding in any way, but nobody ever took advantage of her, and we mixed our work with pleasure and got the job at hand finished. Although we were always kidding her, no one can say we did not obey her. Whenever she would say, "Will someone call me a cab?" we all shouted, "You're a cab!"

The fact that everyone called Ruth "Mother" just came about naturally. I think Bill Thall was the first to call her "Mother," and it stuck like glue. Ruth was always ready to help anyone and all of the staff at WLW. She was constantly being called upon to save a job, or intercede for someone, or just settle a problem, and there were many problems large and small. I vowed I would never call Ruth "Mother" because I was almost as old as she, but soon I had joined the ranks without even knowing.

People's reactions to Ruth always interested me. I used to love to watch the studio audience as Ruth entered for the show. Such happiness was indescribable. On our remotes, as we drove into different cities, and during shopping trips, everyone seeing Ruth would have the look of great recognition of an old friend. The maintenance crew at the station loved her very much and always inquired about her. One of them, speaking in broken English, came to my office with tears in his eyes after learning Ruth was ill to inquire about her health. He said, "She is like a queen," and although he

truly Cincinnati's good-will ambassador. Wherever he traveled, whenever he was introduced as Mayor of Cincinnati, everyone retorted with, "How's Ruth Lyons?" She was known all over the United States, not only to show people, but people in all walks of life, and this always helped him break the ice, so to speak, when he met new people. Lisa Kirk told me she would do anything in the world for Ruth; Johnny Mathis dearly loved Ruth and said her words to him had helped him over a very serious crisis in his life.

We all met many wonderful people working for Ruth, not only the celebrities, but many people who worked behind the scenes. One of my favorites is Charlie Pomeranz. He is a Hollywood agent who never ceased to be amazed over the drawing power that Ruth had when his clients appeared here. Charlie once brought in a group of Hollywood beauties to the "Fifty-Fifty Club" who were to appear on a Jack Benny Special. He told me later that the ratings for this show here in Ruth's territory were simply fantastic. He also brought Celeste Holm on several occasions, and Ruth and Celeste became great friends. They were alike in many respects— both warm hearted toward their fellow man, both quick to defend the race or religion of someone else, both deeply involved in charitable work, both wonderful human beings.

One of the most inspired guests Ruth had was Adela Rogers St. Johns. It was hard to say whether she inspired Ruth or Ruth inspired Adela, but Adela told me she thought Ruth was a person one might meet only once in a lifetime, a real individual who was able to use her freedom on the air for the betterment of the world. This she did. Ask Ethel Waters, or Oscar Robertson, or Celeste Holm, or Waite Hoyt, or ask the lady down the street, or the grocer, or ask the child coming home from the hospital.

Waite Hoyt, the sportscaster for the Cincinnati Reds for

twenty-five years, had known Ruth for many years, and he loved to stop in Ruth's office when he did a show at WLW. He would call for "Mother," and that was really something, for if Ruth was old enough to be his mother, she must be very, very old. He delighted in teasing Ruth and always let her know when it was Senior Citizens Day at the ball park. It was sometimes difficult for Waite to get past all of us to see Ruth, and he would tell her, "Golly, you have more people working for you than Shillito's!" In a serious moment, Waite wrote of Ruth, "Doubtlessly the finest and most beloved personality in television—bar all others. I am proud and privileged to be counted among her friends."

Paul Dixon told me several times of his feeling for Ruth, and he always loved to talk of her kindness to him when he was so ill for so many weeks. I shall never forget the day someone came into the office and said, "Paul Dixon is ill and they have him on the bed in the lounge on the fourth floor." Without a word Ruth flew out of the office, as though she had wings on her feet, to Paul's side. Paul complained of pains in his chest, and at first Ruth wanted to use her favorite home remedy, Bengue, but she saw it was something really serious, so sent for a doctor and an ambulance in a hurry. Paul told me that as he lay there week after week, he became more and more depressed and feared for the worst. The doctors urged him to get out of bed and walk, but he simply could not. One day Ruth arrived, and hearing of his plight was determined to help. She said, "Come on, Paul, we're going for a walk." She insisted, and Paul finally obeyed, and they walked up and down the hall. I can just picture them, that big hulk of a man leaning on that little 5'2" blonde, but they did it together, and that was the beginning of Paul's miraculous recovery. "And, Gloria," Paul said, "Ruth was the only person who came to me and asked if I needed any financial assistance when I was sick—and I'll never forget that."

Many times during the summer and on holidays, Ruth brought a dear little girl to work with her. Candy was thirteen when I started to work for Ruth, and I saw her blossom from an adorable little girl into a lovely young lady. She, like her father, Herman Newman, always stayed in the background. Though Herman rarely came to the show, his presence was felt, for he is a true humanitarian and his love for the dignity of man was often felt in many of the ideas Ruth conveyed. What Ruth never knew is that all of her secretaries had a crush on her husband.

We all admired Candy, for she was the most thoughtful person, and I often feel she made all of us more thoughtful and understanding of each other. Candy was sincere and a deep thinker, always weighing every question before she gave her opinion. She was a happy person and appreciated the finer things of life. We loved to tease Candy because she liked to laugh and especially to laugh at herself, and she kidded back, but she was always careful never to hurt anyone. Candy and I had several things in common. We both loved antiques, animals, and the study of history, although I liked American history, and she was an expert on European history. She made a special trip to my office to see me every day, and I am sure she did the same for the other girls.

Candy was truly a joy to her mother and father. Everyone knows how Ruth loved Candy because it came through with every word that Ruth uttered about her, but Candy also adored her mother and worshipped her. I had never seen so much devotion, and when Ruth was ill, Candy did so much to help make her mother well again. No one was to know then how the pendulum would swing back, and it would be Ruth's and Herman's turn to help Candy in her courageous battle against cancer. I can never describe the sadness that prevailed in our office the day following that black June 19, and the next day, and the many to follow. All had the same question on their minds. How could this happen to dear little Candy, how could Ruth and Herman, who had worked so long for and with young people, lose their beloved daughter? Why, why, why . . . ? Thousands of letters rolled in with condolences and about $12,000 for the Christmas Fund in memory of Candy. They were beautiful letters with beautiful thoughts, but I could find no help in them, I could find no answer—I hope Ruth and Herman were able to.

Nobody could ever know the despair in my heart when Ruth told me she could no longer go on in television. Even though we knew it was coming, we could not accept it. I guess we all thought Ruth Lyons would go on forever. Everyone was so happy on that day in January. Ruth had just returned from a Christmas cruise to Puerto Rico. This followed her final Christmas Fund drive, and we were so glad to have her back. Elsa and Mickey were at a meeting, and Ruth and I were sitting quietly in her office when suddenly Ruth said, "Gloria, I'm going to leave. I just can't go on anymore!" At first I said, "You must go on for your own sake," but then I realized perhaps I was wrong to think this, perhaps we were wrong to urge her on, and I finally realized Ruth really had to give up. We both cried for a while, and then quietly we went downstairs to her cab. Coming back on the elevator, one of the secretaries saw my red and swollen eyes, but she wisely didn't ask any questions. Had it been the reverse, I would have asked what the matter was. When the announcement was finally made, I met the same girl, and she said, "Now I know why you looked so terrible that day."

Of the handful of people who were told Ruth was going to retire, I don't think anyone really believed it except me. I

My four secretaries, three of whom have written in the last chapter, and one who typed my book. From left to right: Elsa Sule, Sue West, Mickey Fisher, Gloria Rush.

knew at last Ruth had to leave. I now wondered if we had done the fair thing to her in urging her to return after Candy's passing, and I wished that we had backed her more when she had wanted to cut down her shows about three years before, but we all selfishly could not give her up, not even for a day a week. But now we would have to. Every day, in those last three weeks, as I watched Ruth in the studio performing, I kept thinking—only nine more shows, only six more, only one more—what would this audience do if they knew . . . ? On Friday, January 20, Carol Channing, though her *Dolly* was sold out in Dayton, came to visit Ruth. This was a fabulous show, and I thought this would be a great show to say farewell, but, no, thank goodness, there were three more shows. And maybe, maybe Ruth could be persuaded to stay, but not by me because I knew we had been too demanding of Ruth now. Ruth told Carol of her plans after the show, and Carol was stricken and said the Midwest would never be the same without her beloved Ruth. How true . . .

On Wednesday, January 25, with the Friday show left, I was concerned and worried as to how Ruth could possibly say good-bye to her devoted audience. In the studio, as the show was on the air, I dared not think that Ruth would sit on that couch only one more day. As soon as we were off the air, the women in the audience surrounded her, and then a crippled lady asked to shake her hand. Everyone was saying such beautiful things to her, as they did so often, and I finally felt it might become too much for her, so I took her hand and led her away, but I do believe she was in much better shape than I was.

Thursday was the day of the big decision. Ruth called and said she had decided she could not say good-bye to her audience in person. Mickey got on the phone, Elsa got on the phone, I got on the phone and insisted she just had to say good-bye herself, but the answer came from Herman. He said absolutely "No," Ruth was not going to do this, as it would be much too hard for her. Thank goodness for his foresight, because we could never have stood it if Ruth had been there. Everyone was crying, Mickey and I were almost in a state of collapse, and the audience, in tears, was so shocked they couldn't move.

There were no phone calls the rest of the afternoon of that fateful day. The management wisely had the switchboard operator cut them off, as we couldn't have taken them, but I really don't think there were many that day anyway, from what I heard later. There was really nothing one could say, and everyone was too stunned to call. Though the fans all knew Ruth's retirement was inevitable, they, like all of us, could hardly accept it. But by the weekend they managed to pull themselves together, for thousands of the most beautiful tear-stained letters began pouring in, each one thanking Ruth for some particular help and the entertainment she had given throughout the years.

When I finally left the building that day, there were several people milling about, those same people who often were there waiting to catch a glimpse of Ruth or receive a friendly wave or handshake. One lady whom I had seen very often rushed up to me, and with tears in her eyes, said, "WLW should inlay her footsteps on this front stairway in gold." It was a beautiful thought. When I returned to WLW for a visit several months ago, I thought of this as I went up those steps—there were no gold footsteps.

Ruth meant so many things to so many people—entertainment to some, inspiration to others, hope to a sick child or an elderly person, sales to a client, profit to the management and sponsors, but to us she meant love and warmth, kindness and understanding, knowledge and good clean fun, courage and determination, leadership and integrity, prestige and honor, but most of all, beauty—beauty of soul, beauty of heart, and beauty of spirit.

And now the good years of radio and television are over, but Ruth is most content in her retirement. I talk to her daily on the phone, and I love to visit her in her beautiful and comfortable old home, and most of all, I love it when she and Herman come to visit me. She helped me and encouraged me to make my decision to go into the antique business and often helps me in the necessities of the business, as she knows much about antiques. For me, things as far as Ruth is concerned, haven't changed too much. As before, like turning on the dial, I pick up the phone, and there she is, the same Ruth Lyons, entertaining, debating, talking frankly the way she always did. There is one exception—no commercials. I truly believe, if Ruth wished, she could walk right back on stage and take up just where she left off—and wouldn't the Midwest rejoice!

Almost everyone who comes into my shop asks, "How's Ruth Lyons?" They all want to talk about Ruth and know if she is well. Occasionally someone comes in and says, "I don't want any antiques. I just want to know how Mother is." Once I said to a woman that I felt so sorry for all of Ruth Lyons' fans because they couldn't see her anymore and that I still had her. The woman quickly retorted, "We still have her too; she belongs to us. We have our memories of her, and nobody can take them away." This was something I hadn't thought about, but she was absolutely right. Yes, you do have her. She still belongs to you.

Epilogue

Now that I have retired, I lead a very quiet, almost secluded life. I often think back on the various things that we discussed on the show: the rise of women and their place in the world; how I disliked the "Star-Spangled Banner" as our national anthem, a song that all people cannot sing, but must be done by a trained soprano, usually with great effort. I preferred "America the Beautiful," and still do. How I abhorred punishing children by whipping them. How I deplored our involvement in Vietnam. How I objected to the song, "I Want a Girl Just Like the Girl That Married Dear Old Dad." I always felt that this song was an insult to a young wife, who probably was struggling to make an apple pie as good as her mother-in-law's. How I hated unkindness to others and cruelty to animals, pompousness, bigotry, and unfair tactics. How I could never forgive the mistreatment of old people, injustice, lying, and using someone else for one's own advantage. How I resented the great deal of money which was spent for outer space, while people here on earth were starving.

How I loved to meet good musicians, wonderful singers, fine comedians, and great actresses and actors. And how much I enjoyed plays, movies, television, and meeting the authors of books that I had read and enjoyed.

And the violent political discussions we used to have in the office after the show was over. And how ridiculous many of the filmed TV commercials were, especially those that were supposed to be filmed by hidden cameras. How we wondered about the whereabouts of Mrs. Paul's husband, who let her do all of the catching and preparation of her Frozen Fish Sticks; about how Mrs. Olsen always just *happened* to be in someone's kitchen and never without a can of Folger's Coffee right at hand. And how we ho-ho-hoed with the Jolly Green Giant—all sponsors of mine.

And how my efforts to get Peter Grant and Cliff Lash married were unsuccessful. (I finally succeeded with Elsa.) How we loved to tease Marian Spelman about saving her used Puffs, another sponsor's product. And how Bonnie Lou murdered the King's English with such charm. And how we loved everything that Ruby sang.

And what a great satisfaction it was to watch the total of the Christmas Fund increase each year. But mostly, I appreciated my wonderful audiences, both seen and unseen.

There are many great people that I wish I might have had the honor and pleasure of meeting during the days gone by. To name a few: Sir Winston Churchill; Adalai Stevenson; that great humanitarian, Dr. Albert Schweitzer; that fine young man who was taken from us so tragically, John F. Kennedy; the late Oscar Hammerstein; that marvelous woman, Helen Keller and her remarkable teacher, Miss Anne Sullivan; the late Fannie Hurst; Pearl Buck; the late Clark Gable; the still-going-strong Bing Crosby; and Maurice Chevalier.

Recently, we sold our lovely old home and moved into a high-rise apartment. From our front windows I can see the